PRAISE FOR *THE*

Enriched with references to an Aladdin
cational experiences and institutions, *The Ladder* encourages parents,
teachers and trainers to think widely and laterally. It is the least we
owe our children – and, for that, we owe Bernie a debt of gratitude.

Alastair Stewart, OBE, journalist

Not only will this book support those working in education, but it will
ultimately transform the career journeys and experiences of young
people everywhere. Packed full of information, tried-and-tested
ideas, reflective tasks and case studies, *The Ladder* is a fantastic
resource that I wish my teachers had read when I was in school!

Gavin Oattes, bestselling author and international keynote speaker

Comprehensive and up to date, *The Ladder* is packed with practical
and achievable suggestions for enhancing careers education from
primary age upwards. Bernie has compiled a wealth of thorough
research and draws on his years of experience working with young
people across the UK. He provides a clear vision for how teachers can
provide effective careers education for their pupils and shares his
passionate belief that all young people should be encouraged – and
enabled – to achieve their potential.

Gemma Hay, Principal Teacher of Citizenship, George Heriot's School

I've known and worked with Andrew 'Bernie' Bernard for years. He
always delivers practical, real-world and down-to-earth advice on
employability and success for students. His new book *The Ladder* is
no exception. A great read full of practical tips for both students and
their teachers.

Lee Jackson, award-winning motivational speaker and author
of *How to Enjoy and Succeed at School and College*

Bernie is an amazing man whose passion has helped develop and
encourage young people to aspire and to be successful, whatever
their background or level of education. His very readable and useful
new book continue   nd enthusiasm to help anyon   throughout
The Ladder.

If you are a school head, a teacher, a careers lead, a parent or a businessperson, then parts, if not all, of this book are for you. It can be used over many years to encourage you and to provide advice, guidance and sources of information. *The Ladder* will help anyone who, like me, believes that we must help encourage and support all young people to develop and then achieve their dreams.

Professor Nigel Adams, Director, Buckingham Enterprise & Innovation Unit (BEIU), University of Buckingham

Life is like a game of snakes and ladders – this book helps students not only to find their ladders but to climb them too. Crammed with research, reflections and insights, *The Ladder* will be an invaluable resource for people helping students to fulfil their potential.

Professor Paul McGee, motivational speaker and *Sunday Times* bestselling author

The Ladder is a brilliant user guide for educators and employers invested in providing young people with opportunities to succeed. Brimming with self-reflection tools and practical and thought-provoking exercises, this is a great book for those of us who have been helped on our own path when we were younger, and are now looking for ideas and support to pay it forward.

Sharon Davies, CEO, Young Enterprise

The Ladder is a must-have manual for all who wish to help students make confident career choices. It is useful, practical, concise and, above all, encouraging and inspiring. It will be loved by career teachers, indeed all teachers, but it is also a valuable 'dip in and dip out' resource full of tools and ideas for every adult wanting to help children and young people to enjoy a successful future. I read *The Ladder* as an employer, a business owner, the chair of an enterprise agency and a patron of a youth enterprise support organisation – and I will be recommending this excellent handbook to all of my colleagues.

I recommend Chapter 2 on the continuum for the acquisition of skills and knowledge (CASK) for every reader, but after that you choose the chapter of tools and ideas relevant to the student you are helping. The book features a number of tools – like the 7 Skills Assessment Sheet (7SAS) and the STAR and GROW models – and they are all clearly and helpfully explained. Most of the tools, ideas and recommendations are new to me, even though I've been interested in employability skills and enterprise education for nearly 30 years. Chapter 10 on 'careers questions' is my favourite and I'll be recommending it to all of my colleagues, ranging from primary school teachers to educators at colleges and universities, especially in the run-up to Global Entrepreneurship Week.

Tony Robinson, OBE, author of *The Happipreneur: Why #MicroBizMatters?*

The
LADDER

Supporting students towards successful futures and confident career choices

Andrew Bernard

ındependent
thinking press

First published by

Independent Thinking Press
Crown Buildings, Bancyfelin, Carmarthen, Wales, SA33 5ND, UK
www.independentthinkingpress.com

and

Independent Thinking Press
PO Box 2223, Williston, VT 05495, USA
www.crownhousepublishing.com

Independent Thinking Press is an imprint of Crown House Publishing Ltd.

First published 2021.

Edited by Ian Gilbert.

Cover image © nmarques74 – stock.adobe.com. Career path illustration, pp. 10–11 © Simon Heath. Young person's head icon, p. 21, p. 41, p. 44 and p. 45 © Sir.Vector – stock.adobe.com. Employer's head icon, p. 21 © Sir.Vector – stock.adobe.com. Peers icon, p. 21 © Sir.Vector – stock.adobe.com. Mortar board icon, p. 28 © blankstock – stock.adobe.com. T-shirt icon, p. 28 © telmanbagirov – stock.adobe.com. Director's chair icon, p. 28 © Amru – stock.adobe.com. Screen icon, p. 28 © Amru – stock.adobe.com. Heart with cross icon, p. 28 © valeriyakozoriz – stock.adobe.com. Chemistry flask icon, p. 28 © dstarky – stock.adobe.com. Book icon, p. 28 © blankstock – stock.adobe.com. Paper and pencil icon, p. 28 © blankstock – stock.adobe.com. Bar graph icon, p. 28 © davooda – stock.adobe.com. Car icon, p. 28 © Paul Kovaloff – stock.adobe.com. Interview icon, p. 28 © Sir.Vector – stock.adobe.com. Hammer and spanner icons, p. 28 © Paul Kovaloff – stock.adobe.com. Shield image, p. 39 © Giraphics – stock.adobe.com.

Chapter 4, various quotes taken from Gatsby Charitable Foundation, Good Career Guidance (London: Gatsby Charitable Foundation, 2014). Available at: https://www.gatsby.org.uk/uploads/education/reports/pdf/gatsby-sir-john-holman-good-career-guidance-2014.pdf. Used with kind permission. p. 33, 7SAS is based on Tony Wagner's research and extract from Global Achievement Gap by Tony Wagner, copyright © 2008. Reprinted by permission of Basic Books, an imprint of Hachette Book Group, Inc. pp. 56–57, extract from Nick Chambers, Elnaz T. Kashefpakdel, Jordan Rehill and Christian Percy, Drawing the Future: Exploring the Career Aspirations of Primary School Children from Around the World (London: Education and Employers, 2018), p. iv. Available at: https://www.educationandemployers.org/wp-content/uploads/2018/01/Drawing-the-Future-FINAL-REPORT.pdf. pp. 61–62 © The Careers & Enterprise Company. Reproduced with their permission. p. 64, extract from Rosemary Bennett, Case Study: 'The Minute I Heard About the BTec I Was Instantly Excited', The Times (24 August). Available at: https://thetimes.co.uk/article/case-study-the-minute-i-heard-about-the-btec-i-was-instantly-excited-plk8nqgzn. © Times, 2019. p. 65, extract from from Sally Weale, Poorer Pupils Twice as Likely to Fail Key GCSEs, The Guardian (21 August 2019). Available at: https://www.theguardian.com/education/2019/aug/21/poorer-pupils-twice-as-likely-to-fail-key-gcses © Guardian News & Media Ltd, 2020. pp. 92–93, © NCW, from a selection of resources available at https://ncw2020.co.uk/. Reproduced with their permission. pp. 136–139 © Anita Devi, 2021.

British Library Cataloguing-in-Publication Data
A catalogue entry for this book is available from the British Library.

Print ISBN 978-178135374-5
Mobi ISBN 978-178135382-0
ePub ISBN 978-178135383-7
ePDF ISBN 978-178135384-4

LCCN 2020951724

Printed and bound in the UK by
Charlesworth Press, Wakefield, West Yorkshire

PREFACE

I started writing this book in July 2019 and now it is September 2020. The majority of the global population has been affected by the COVID-19 pandemic in 2020 and the consequences are sure to be far-reaching and long-term.

In June 2020 the World Bank issued a stark set of forecasts and warnings for the future economic prosperity of the majority of the globe, saying, 'While the ultimate outcome is still uncertain, the pandemic will result in contractions across the vast majority of emerging market and developing economies.'[1] The bank predicts that 'global coordination and cooperation will be critical' to recovery. Their baseline forecast suggests the likelihood of a '5.2 percent contraction in global GDP', which they confirm is the 'deepest global recession in decades'.

This book was written to support schools in giving their young people the best possible future by helping them create their ladder to success. That ladder is based on understanding, developing and sharing their skills alongside more formal learning and qualifications.

It looks as though this book has been written at just the right time.

As my final edits are completed, the Careers and Enterprise Company have released some topical research into teachers' thoughts about the future, post-COVID-19. Gathering the views of nearly 5,000 teachers using a Teacher Tapp survey, they found that 74% of teachers believe that employability skills will be the most important way to improve students' career prospects in the near future.[2] Additionally, the survey found that almost half (49%) fear there will be 'far fewer jobs and opportunities for their students in the coming years'.

It's true to say that no one can predict exactly what the long-term effects of the COVID-19 pandemic will be, but one thing seems certain: it's going to be much harder to find work as companies reduce their workforces or are forced to close. It seems that it has never

---

1 See https://www.worldbank.org/en/publication/global-economic-prospects.
2 Careers and Enterprise Company, Workplace skills now more important than exam results in post-Covid jobs market say teachers (7 July 2020). Available at: https://www.careersandenterprise.co.uk/news/workplace-skills-now-more-important-exam-results-post-covid-jobs-market-say-teachers.

been more important to highlight all the options that are open to young people and the various ways in which they can get there.

With the creativity and adaptability apparent in young people, I foresee a generation of people who will rethink the way they look at their skills and abilities and how they relate to employment, self-employment and entrepreneurship.

I truly hope this book helps you to help them.

FOREWORD BY
COLONEL DAME KELLY HOLMES

I wouldn't be who I am unless my PE teacher gave me the opportunity to change, by telling me that I could be good at something – running – and encouraging me to pursue that as a sport.

My teacher really supported me and continued to push me to focus on my sporting goals during my school years. I wasn't really academic at all and being in athletics gave me a sense of identity and purpose. This helped me to set my dreams and formed the basis of my career.

I always believe that if you can help someone to change by giving them an opportunity to see for themselves that they can succeed, then that will never be forgotten by them, or by you. This, I suppose, is the essence of what every teacher and adult can do to support young people to develop their vision of themselves in the future.

I know that sport has a wonderful ability to unite and bring people together, especially if they believe their only avenue to self-expression is sport. This gives people the opportunity to develop a variety of skills: interacting and socialising, communicating with others and taking part allows you to learn life lessons. Failure isn't the end, it's the chance to translate a negative into wanting to change, improve and better yourself.

Whatever it is you go through in life and whatever it is you want to achieve, I believe you should try to find your diamond – the skills or quality that sets you apart - then you can go all the way. Sometimes it's harder to find that diamond within yourself, but those who do will find they are able to push through to another level.

Whatever you do in life, we all need a champion – someone to help us try to find our diamond. Will you join me and Bernie to help young people find their diamonds?

Kelly x

ACKNOWLEDGEMENTS

This book would not be in your hands without the support, friendship and kindness of the following people.

My family: Val, my wife, the strongest of women, who raises my sights, holds me to account and us all together; Millie and Ruby, the most incredible women, who I'm lucky enough to call my daughters. x

Friends who have played parts in my journey in many ways and at different times: Paul Wilson, Ian Clarkson, David and Debs Hurst, Joe McLoughlin, Tony Burrows, Jules Walker, Gema Ensenat, the Leaf family, Zak Croft, Matt Kerslake, Heather Heaton Gallagher, the Mousley family, Nicola Hall and Gemma Hay.

Clients and colleagues who've become friends: Steph Boyle and Nicola Crowther at the Manufacturing Institute, Amy Leonard and the team at The Talent Foundry; Jane Rawnsley, Taslima Khatun and Alison Westhead at the Prudential; Colonel Dame Kelly Holmes; Sarah Glass and the team at the Centre for Leadership Performance.

Nick Newman, Stephen Logan, Ken McCall, Ross Bennett and the ambassadors and partners at National Careers Week (NCW): every year you amaze me with what we achieve. Teamwork.

Fellow speakers at the Professional Speaking Association of the UK and Ireland, especially Sarah Fox and Lee Jackson.

Our school clients – some of whom have been with Innovative Enterprise for over a decade – who continue to have faith in our ability to inspire and support students.

Ian Gilbert at Independent Thinking and David Bowman, Louise Penny, Bev Randell and the team at Crown House Publishing for having the faith in me to write this book.

My friends on Twitter, many of whom I've never met, who daily make me laugh, and to think and debate education, well-being, politics, careers and kindness. Join me: @EnterpriseSBox.

Young people who continue to impress, surprise and amaze me ... and often really, really, really make me laugh.

Thank you all, you've all played a part in making this book what it is.

CONTENTS

GLOSSARY

7SAS   Seven Skills Assessment Sheet

ACEs   adverse childhood experiences

BAME   black and minority ethnic[1]

BTEC   Business and Technology Education Council (UK qualification awarding body – awarding HNCs, HNDs and other diplomas of a technical nature)

CASK   continuum for the acquisition of skills and knowledge

CBI   Confederation of British Industry

CEIAG   careers education, information, advice and guidance

CIC   community interest company

CMI   Chartered Management Institute

CSR   corporate social responsibility

CV   curriculum vitae

DBS   Disclosure and Barring Service

EAL   English as an additional language

EHCPs   education, health and care plans

FE   further education

HE   higher education

HESA   Higher Education Statistics Agency

---

1   During the 2020 Black Lives Matter protests, sparked by the unlawful killing of George Floyd in Minnesota, USA, there has been much debate on this side of the Atlantic about the catch-all/shorthand term 'BAME'. Many people who could be described as such feel it is a demeaning term, a term that 'others' people of colour. My use of the acronym in this book reflects its use in many pieces of research or projects from organisations which support people of colour. It is not for me to challenge or debate the use of this label in the course of this book. I have also reflected on changing the descriptor to 'people of colour' or 'non-white', but again these are problematic terms – especially non-white, which I feel is even more 'othering'.
    The slightly uncomfortable compromise I have reached, therefore, is to maintain the use of BAME where relevant but to acknowledge that it will jar with some readers. For this I apologise.

HNC   BTEC Higher National Certificate

HND   BTEC Higher National Diploma

LEP   Local Enterprise Partnership

LMI   labour market information

MAT   multi-academy trust

NEET   not in education, employment or training

NCOP   National Collaborative Outreach Programme (UK
         university scheme)

NCS   National Careers Service

NCW   National Careers Week

OFFA   Office for Fair Access

PCA   parent careers association

PESTLE   political, economic, social, technological, legal and
         environmental factors

PSHEE   personal, social, health and economic education

PTA   parent–teacher association

SEND   special educational needs and disabilities

SLT   senior leadership team

SME   small and medium sized enterprise (in the UK, less than
         250 employees and under £50 million turnover)

STEAM   science, technology, engineering, arts, maths

STEM   science, technology, engineering, maths

UCAS   Universities and Colleges Admissions Service

UTC   university technical college

NOTE FOR TEACHERS, MENTORS AND ADVISORS

Life is short and moves quickly. Decisions (or the lack thereof) can affect you for many years, and in the context of careers we often don't realise what we 'should have been' until it feels like it's too late. When reflecting on the life paths we've chosen, we will often realise that random opportunities lead to interesting journeys and, in the end, make us who we are. But what if we had had help in making better decisions earlier on?

Using the mantra that 'every adult is a careers teacher', this book aims to inspire and support educators and education leaders to explicitly link their subject area(s) to students' futures in and outside school. There are plenty of free, effective and easy-to-use ideas to help you to support them in this book and referred to or signposted throughout it.

Who should read this book?

Adults who were helped by someone when they were younger, whatever their position now. (So, everyone then.)

More specifically:

- Teachers: secondary heads of year and subject leaders.
- Secondary school head teachers and members of the senior leadership team (SLT).
- Careers leaders and guidance professionals.
- Employees, managers and directors in businesses and other organisations.
- Further education (FE) and higher education (HE) lecturers and tutors.
- Governors.
- Parents.

This book supports educators to empower students in another crucial dimension: attitude. I want to help you to support children through changes in their beliefs about themselves and what they're capable of. The journey looks something like:

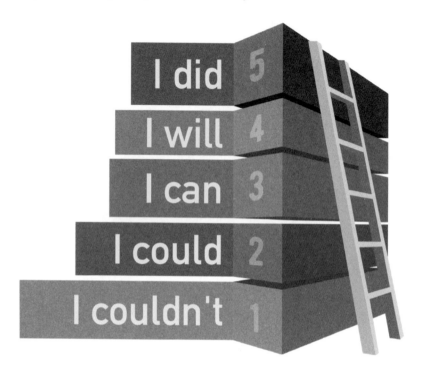

It's important that teachers support students' aspirations and help them with future thinking (tempered with, but not crushed by, realism). Do you know anyone who won't sing in public because 'someone said I was tone deaf', or someone who gave up on their ideal career because a teacher said 'you'll never make the grades for that', or someone who didn't go to university because a parent or family member said 'that's not for people like us'?

So, here's what we can do instead: help them to bring the future to life. This book contains all you need to know in order to be an advocate for young people and their future aspirations, pathways and career aims.

Chapter 1

YOU ARE HERE

The longer I live, the more convinced I become that life is 10% what happens to us and 90% how we react to it.

Charles R. Swindoll[1]

How did you get to where you are today?

Did you have a clear plan for your schooling, work, career, family and relationships?

Did everything go to plan?

Did life take a few turns you weren't expecting?

Perhaps there were a couple of 'random occurrences' you couldn't have planned?

Did you do it all on your own?

I'm willing to bet that your life has been defined by a series of decisions (some more considered than others), a few periods of comfort, a couple of sparks of pure chance and some drifting, as well as some support from others when you needed it, even if that was unsolicited because you didn't realise you needed it. Sound familiar?

This book is an exploration of the positive effects of random occurrences and how they can shape and change the direction of our lives. More importantly, it's an exploration of how we can use our positions and experiences to create more, seemingly random, such occurrences to support young people as they explore and progress their education, careers and lives.

---

1   Charles R. Swindoll, *Strengthening Your Grip* (London: Hodder and Stoughton, 1982), p. 206.

My journey

Officially my name is Andrew David Bernard, but to be honest I don't really like the name Andrew. At school, where all my friends had a nickname, I was called Bernie. Seeing as everyone who knows me calls me this, and I reckon it suits me, I call myself Bernie. Hello.

I was brought up in Buckinghamshire, England, where I lived with my dad, David, mum, Jean, and sister, Sarah Jane. I went to a grammar school where I was one of only two boys from my primary school to get a place. (My parents moved to a new house to be in the catchment area.) They said I was 'lucky'; however, it didn't feel like it. I wasn't particularly happy there – especially as all my close friends had gone to the secondary modern nearby. I grinned (mostly) and bore it.

During my early teens I was becoming an accomplished cyclist, winning the chance to compete in a national competition. I did not, however, end up riding in the nationals, because my bike was stolen. Well, that's the reason I gave to anyone who asked; on reflection, I think I was looking for an excuse not to be humiliated on the national stage, so used this one. It has always been a huge regret.

Alongside my sporting endeavours, my O-level (as they were in those days) results were OK – 9 in total, all Bs and Cs – but then at 16 there was another choice: sixth form, college or work? By this point I'd made some good friends at school and they were pretty much all going to the local college to study A levels. Me? Well, my parents decided that I would 'do better' if I stayed at the grammar to do mine. As you can imagine, this wasn't what I'd hoped for, but there was no winning mum and dad round to my way of thinking. Unfortunately, like many teenagers who don't get their way, I decided that life was not fair and embarked on a full-blown two-year tantrum fuelled by machismo, anger, testosterone and entitlement.

It did not go well and after two years of coasting, arguing, showing off[2] and generally being angry, results day arrived. Many of my schoolmates were jumping around shouting happily about how they'd got into Oxford, Cambridge, Durham or LSE. I slunk off home with the unopened envelope containing the results for the two A levels I had completed. When I opened it, after a minute of disbelief, I experienced

---

2 'For every boy who tries to succeed, there is another boy who tries to fail. [...] Sometimes, they try too hard to impress popular peers and forget about trying to impress their teachers.' Matt Pinkett and Mark Roberts, *Boys Don't Try? Rethinking Masculinity in Schools* (Abingdon and New York: Routledge, 2019), p. 1.

the first genuine emotion I'd felt for years, maybe ever. I started bawling my eyes out as I realised that I'd wasted the past two years, with only an E in sociology and a U in business studies to my name. Well, despite *thinking* I knew it all, I honestly had *no* idea what to do.

In the end, I did something I'd not done for years – I asked for help. Specifically, I asked my mum for help in trying to find a course that would take me – I didn't care where or doing what, I just needed to break the toxic chains I'd wrapped myself in, go away and grow up. Despite my U grade in business studies, I decided that a course in business, or business and finance, would be a good one for me as a broad-brush approach to future career options. I couldn't face exploring other subjects at this low point, and business was some-thing I already knew a little bit about.

There were two BTEC Higher National Diploma (HND) business stud-ies courses on offer that I could apply for: at Huddersfield Polytechnic and North East Wales Institute of Higher Education (NEWI). I was offered an interview for both, but the one at NEWI happened to be first. When the letter arrived offering me a place I said, 'That'll do.'

'That'll do' is *not* what you usually (or, indeed, should) say when you're deciding on the next steps of your education or career, but I'd left myself with very little choice. Still, I never even went to Huddersfield for the interview. Fast-forward 20 years and, after leav-ing north Wales with a distinction in business and finance and a career path which was anything but logical, I was living in Lancashire, married and with a young family. I had a single thought as I left work at Lancaster University one winter's day: the doors slid open and the cold air hit me in the face and I thought, 'That's the best part of my day.' That's when I realised that I was *very* unhappy with the work I had been doing. My role in business development was an extremely important part of the university, but it wasn't something that made my heart sing. In fact, it made me stressed, anxious and unhappy.

At 38 I had my first serious thoughts about what I wanted to do ... 20 years after leaving school. My doctor signed me off work due to stress and my wife Val (a counsellor and therapist) got to work. We used the Wheel of Life (which we'll learn all about on page 40) and instantly saw what was wrong – it was work and career plans and how they impacted on my happiness and feelings of usefulness. She asked me when I was last truly happy. Bear in mind Val's my wife so I needed to think carefully. I took a full 10 minutes to sheepishly (and honestly) reply with: 'On that French campsite in August when we had that big mad game of football with those 30 kids.' She smiled and said: 'I knew you were going to say that. You need to work with young people.' A week later, Innovative Enterprise was born.

It had taken me 38 years to find my purpose! *Thirty-eight years!*

Simply, this led me to become the person I most needed when I was younger, and so enterprise, attitude and aspiration became the themes around which I built and designed workshops. Fifteen years on and we've worked with more than 150,000 young people and hundreds of businesses.

So what? So, I want to distil what I've learned, what's worked and what has helped young people, teachers, schools and businesses and bring together those insights for you to put into practice. I want to show you how you can help the young people you teach, mentor, support, parent and guide to find skills, attitudes and purpose that will bring them success and happiness.

I grew up in Britain in the 1970s and 1980s, a time of Thatcher, the closure of the pits and steelworks, strikes, and yuppies and 'big business' making millions at the expense of 'ordinary jobs'. The last thing I wanted to be was an entrepreneur, an owner of 'the forces of production', yet here we are. I have run my own business since 2006.

Chance, opportunities and openings aren't always predictable. When I was asked to do a TEDx Talk, I decided to call it 'Engineering Random Opportunities to Succeed'.[3] If we can create random opportunities (meaning occurrences that young people would never or hardly ever come across ordinarily) then there are more chances for sparks of inspiration and interest to be created and new directions to be pursued. I believe that it's *essential* that we create as many random opportunities as possible for young people at all stages of their journeys of personal discovery – in and out of educational settings. Just one of these experiences can change and improve someone's vision for themselves, their direction, their goals and, ultimately, their life.

---

3 Andrew Bernard, 'Engineering Random Opportunities to Succeed', *TEDxWhitehaven* (14 October 2016). Available at: https://youtu.be/BILhkke2sfQ.

Steve Jobs, founder of Apple, said:

You can't connect the dots looking forward; you can only connect them looking backwards. So you have to trust that the dots will somehow connect in your future. You have to trust in something – your gut, destiny, life, karma, whatever.[4]

I see it as my place in the world to inspire and create the dots, the chances, the new and different opportunities to help young people discover themselves: what makes them tick, what makes their hearts sing and what helps them to stand out in a world that is trying to make them fit in. Because I wasted (invested?) 17 years in the wrong jobs, I've made it my mission to support young people in whatever way I can, and that's why I wrote this book. Wherever you are now, you probably took a long time and a circuitous path to get there. I'm hoping that you too will want to help young people take a more direct path to their future success and happiness.

Self-reflection task

Think about your career path.

Was it all planned?

Was it affected by 'life getting in the way'?

Draw out your career path on a large sheet of paper. Start in the bottom left as you leave school and aim to finish in the top right, with any changes of plan or direction reflected in your pathway. If you like you can draw images to illustrate your journey. You can share these on Twitter and Instagram when you've finished, using #SetUpTheLadder.

---

4   Steve Jobs, Stanford University Commencement Speech, 12 June 2005. Available at: https://news.stanford.edu/2005/06/14/jobs-061505/.

Here is a representation of my career path, designed by the wonderful Simon Heath.[5]

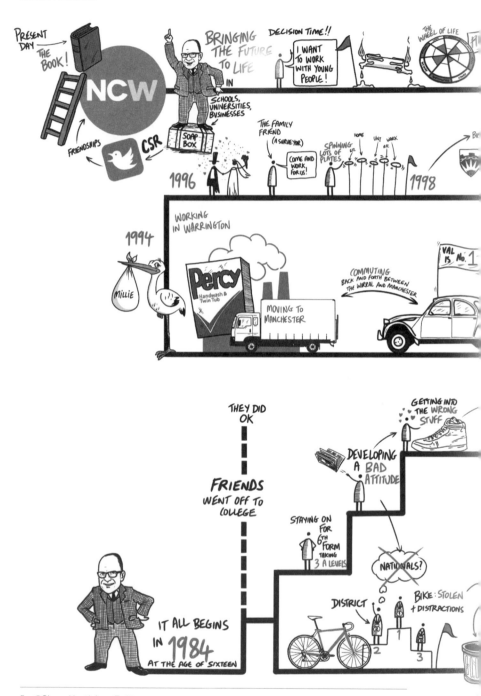

5   @SimonHeath1 on Twitter.

How this book works

I want this book to be *used*, so I've made the materials within it user-friendly, fun and engaging for educators and the young people they work with.

You will find:

- Resources that can be adapted for integration into different subject areas and to suit your students and their ambitions.
- Tools that allow careers guidance and inspiration to be included and embedded in subject areas and provide ways to maintain relevance as the job market, and the world, changes.
- Tools to help young people see their skills and abilities objectively *and* record, describe and be proud of them.
- Tools to help young people discover their purpose.
- Tools to help with applications and personal statements as well as interviews.
- Tools to make careers research and future planning more engaging for everybody.
- Self-reflection tasks – exercises to develop your own awareness.
- Case studies – best practice examples for inspiration and signposting, including suggestions for how partnerships with businesses can help to support young people.
- Research that explores inequality of opportunity and why careers and future-focused work is so crucial.
- Plans for developing careers learning across educational establishments.
- Questions to ask, for anyone involved in the careers and enterprise development of young people.
- Downloadable resources.

This book is a collation of experiences and learning collected through hundreds of careers and enterprise activities I've led, designed and been involved with: best practice ideas; research on careers and corporate social responsibility (CSR); and developmental activities and resources I've created and used in my business practice. It also brings in voices and research from employers, third-sector organisations, and other educators and experts in careers education and employability.

Careers advice continues (or should continue) to evolve as work-places change, technology changes, education changes and opportunities change. Different industries will need people with different skills and abilities as emergent technology – artificial intelligence, robotisation, 5G – and advances in logistics and manu-facturing change the way the workforce interacts with one another, their equipment and their clients. All the classic PESTLE – political, economic, social, technological, legal and environmental – factors come into play at some point or another during learning, working and living.

In the UK, recent and current political and social changes (yes, Brexit – which at the time of writing is supposed to have been 'done' by 31 January 2020, but which in reality will take at least a year of further negotiating and then another decade or more of wrangling) will have short-, medium- and, very likely, long-term impacts on employment levels in the UK, and knock-on impacts for education and society at large for decades to come. Despite promises of 'sunlit uplands', there seems to be relatively few apparent benefits.

This book is being edited during the COVID-19 global pandemic: lockdown continues in certain areas, schools remained open for key workers' children and there were no examinations in summer 2020 – so grades were (eventually) calculated by teachers based on previous internal assessments as well as mock exam data. It seems that this book will be more useful than ever in helping future students understand and be able to explain their skills, qualities, attitudes and behaviours alongside their grades – whether examined or calculated.

This book will assist educators in secondary schools, in particular, to support young people in gathering information about careers, con-sidering the available pathways, and finding the inspiration and motivation to develop the skills and achieve the qualifications they need in order to fulfil their potential. I hope that the book serves as a handbook of ideas for the non-careers teacher to ensure that future thinking is built into all subjects in ways which are relatively simple: my aim is that this approach shouldn't add very much to already full workloads.

You may know people who work in a business, charity or other setting whose role it is to support, recruit and/or develop young people. This book is for them, too – schools and students really benefit from the input of employers and outside organisations to bring their futures to life and support inspiration and transition into the world of work. In fact, young people who have meaningful encounters with employers and career inspiration are much less likely to become a not in education employment or training (NEET) statistic.[6]

I firmly believe that careers advice is as crucial to young people as pastoral support and well-being interventions are. Careers advice is *vital* to a student's life chances as it helps to broaden their vision of what they *could* become. As one head teacher who was interviewed in Ofsted's *Getting Ready for Work* report said:

We wish to raise the aspiration and broaden the horizons of our students by giving them a real experience of the world of work before they leave school. For many of our students their world is very narrow and this [work experience] is an opportunity to mix with people beyond their own community. It also begins to embed some of the real world skills, which students need.[7]

Whilst school, importantly, focuses on academic learning and success, the future can be made more exciting, less narrow and more filled with possibility through a broad range of careers learning and discussions. As my National Careers Week (NCW) co-director and deputy head teacher friend Stephen Logan said to me in an email:

All schools should do careers education because it's the right thing to do. [...] Careers in a school connects everything from the curriculum, teaching, leading and pedagogy. Everyday conversation and interaction is preparing young people for their future, whether it be through raising expectations, aspirations, ambitions and challenges, it is our moral obligation and purpose to provide high-quality CEIAG [careers education, information, advice and guidance] for all.

I couldn't agree more.

6 Anthony Mann, It's Who You Meet: Why Employer Contacts at School Make a Difference to the Employment Prospects of Young Adults. Education and Employers Taskforce, 2012. Available at: https://www.educationandemployers.org/wp-content/uploads/2014/06/its_who_you_meet_final_26_06_12.pdf.
7 Ofsted, *Getting Ready for Work*. Ref: 160056 (November 2016), p. 12. Available at: https://assets.publishing.service.gov.uk/government/uploads/system/uploads/attachment_data/file/577236/Getting_ready_for_work.pdf.

This book will help embed careers education *alongside* the academic, sporting and social elements of schools, colleges and universities, as it should be.

The Department for Education published statutory guidance in October 2018 which stated that:

A successful careers guidance programme will also be reflected in higher numbers of pupils progressing to positive destinations such as apprenticeships, technical routes, school sixth forms, sixth form colleges, further education colleges, universities or employment.[8]

I advocate a simple yet powerful approach which should ensure that education leaders can embed broader careers knowledge and future learning throughout their establishment: school should not be seen as just a procession towards university.

This book's main structural feature is the continuum for the acquisition of skills and knowledge (CASK), which I've created to highlight how we acquire different skills and knowledge at different times of our lives. This knowledge and skill blend is tested and certificated in different ways – think about your first spelling tests, earning badges at Scouts or Guides, certificates for swimming and athletics – inside and outside the school environment: GCSEs, A levels, HNDs, driving tests, and first aid and safety certificates at work. The CASK is described in Chapter 2 and is augmented with a series of tools that have been developed and used in a variety of workshops and programmes through my organisation, Innovative Enterprise: some with NCW and with partners in many different settings, others created especially for this book.

Surrounding and supporting the CASK are some tools to help with measuring personal skills acquisition and organisational success in embedding activities to support careers and personal development.

---

8   Department for Education, *Careers Guidance and Access for Education and Training Providers: Statutory Guidance for Governing Bodies, School Leaders and School Staff.* Ref: DFE-00002-2018 (October 2018), p. 6. Available at: https://assets.publishing.service.gov.uk/government/uploads/system/uploads/attachment_data/file/748474/181008_schools_statutory_guidance_final.pdf.

The two most significant references used in developing the CASK were:

- The seven survival skills for careers, college and citizenship from *The Global Achievement Gap* by Dr Tony Wagner.[9]

- *Good Career Guidance*: The Gatsby Charitable Foundation[10] (known as the Gatsby Benchmarks) issued in 2014 and referenced in the Department for Education's *Careers Strategy*[11] and statutory guidance.[12]

Self-reflection task

Think about the careers advice you received.

Assuming that (a) you had some and (b) you can remember it, what were you told?

When was this conversation had in your school or college? At which stage of your learning journey?

Did you get the feeling you were prepared for it?

Do you remember knowing about any of your skills and what you enjoyed?

Did it help you to decide what (or what not) to do as a career and the processes you needed to follow to get there?

Did it leave you feeling positive and ready for the world of work?

9 Tony Wagner, *The Global Achievement Gap: Why Even Our Best Schools Don't Teach the New Survival Skills Our Children Need – and What We Can Do About It* (New York: Basic Books, 2008).

10 Gatsby Charitable Foundation, *Good Career Guidance* (London: Gatsby Charitable Foundation, 2014). Available at: https://www.gatsby.org.uk/uploads/education/reports/pdf/gatsby-sir-john-holman-good-career-guidance-2014.pdf.

11 Department for Education, *Careers Strategy: Making the Most of Everyone's Skills and Talents*. Ref: DFE-00310-2017 (December 2017), p. 18. Available at: https://assets.publishing.service.gov.uk/government/uploads/system/uploads/attachment_data/file/664319/Careers_strategy.pdf.

12 Department for Education, *Careers Guidance and Access for Education and Training Providers*, p. 6.

You're not going to get tested, but just jot down your ideas and reflect on the usefulness or otherwise of the advice you were offered. Ask around amongst your friends, colleagues and family – I bet you get some great stories!

For the record

Teachers are incredibly hard-working. They need to know their subject inside out, recognise hundreds of children, read dozens of emails every day and remain professional and implacable in the face of the vagaries of childhood self-expression, teenage hormones and parental, let's call it, 'interest'. I am reminded of the oft-quoted sentiment: 'Summer holidays: when parents realise just how underpaid teachers really are.' This was also the case when parents had to homeschool their children during the closure of schools due to the COVID-19 lockdown.

To expect teachers to keep up with the rapidly accelerating changes in the employability market, industry, Technology 2.0, 2.26 or 3.0, the Fourth Industrial Revolution, etc. is not only unreasonable, it's also impractical. This book will help all subject and pastoral teachers with ideas and signposting to make their work a bit easier with regard to careers, enterprise, and personal, social, health and economic (PSHEE) learning.

I'm not advocating that we turn school into some sort of treadmill into work through judgements based on how useful a child will be to the economy in later life. I am advocating that we embark on the habit of linking learning in the classroom, science lab, sports field or drama studio explicitly to the skills and knowledge that will benefit our young people and society in the future.

Businesses' concerns that young people are not work-ready when they leave school are often reported in the media and in studies into employability. On average in England, 36% of employers surveyed thought 16-year-olds were 'poorly or very poorly' prepared for work; 29% thought 17–18-year-olds entering their first full-time job were 'poorly or very poorly' prepared for work.[13] This may have been a valid comment in Victorian times when schools existed either to ready the population for agriculture, labouring, factory or 'below stairs' work or to prepare individuals to lead and manage others.

Times have changed, and because the role of school is to provide education and inspiration for the many pathways of the future it's reasonable to expect that businesses who would like 'work-ready' young people in an ever-changing world should contribute to keeping them up to date with that changing world, isn't it? Nigel Whitehead, chief technology officer at BAE Systems in the UK, says:

Businesses and employees can no longer believe it is another business's responsibility to train and upskill the workforce of the future. [...] I believe personal and corporate responsibility, collaboration and sharing best practice are key to solving these issues.[14]

I fully agree, Nigel.

I want *every* employer (and ideally every employee) to support at least one young person in their careers education each year. Imagine harnessing that much knowledge, information and enthusiasm. Imagine ...

In a recent study by Warwick University, Sally-Anne Barnes et al. found that 40% of parents felt ill-equipped to advise on careers:

Recent surveys of parents and students reported that just three in five parents felt confident in advising their child about 'how they can achieve their career/job goals' or 'what career/job options would be best for them'.[15]

13 Careers and Enterprise Company, *Prioritisation Index 2015: Cold Spots* (2015). Data from table, p. 13. Available at: https://www.careersandenterprise.co.uk/sites/default/files/uploaded/cold_spots_report_2015.pdf.

14 BAE Systems, *Future Skills for Our UK Business: A Whitepaper* (June 2019), p. 4. Available at: https://www.baesystems.com/en/our-company/skills-and-education/future-skills-for-our-uk-business.

15 Sally-Anne Barnes, Jenny Bimrose, Alan Brown, John Gough and Sally Wright, *The Role of Parents and Carers in Providing Careers Guidance and How They Could Be Better Supported* (Warwick: University of Warwick, 2020), p. 1. Available at: https://warwick.ac.uk/fac/soc/ier/research/careerguidanceparents/ier_gatsby_jpm_parents-carers_final_report_v8_final.pdf.

Many parents often base their advice on their own career/work experiences ... which are likely to be out of date and affected by their experiences of school and of careers advice. By harnessing the power of employers, educators *and* parents we can better equip young people to make informed, current and relevant choices when it comes to considering their future careers. There is no one-size-fits-all career plan to meet the needs of all the young people in the UK, Europe or globally: by opening up opportunities for young people to learn about, experience and gain a flavour of different roles and skills, finding a suitable and fulfilling career should be achievable for all.

I subscribe to the idea that all of us have a purpose for being on the earth – a skill, a talent, a reason to be, a way of behaving that makes the heart sing and brings a smile to the face. Purpose can sometimes come to us in the natural course of our daily lives: something we notice about society that needs to be changed or something we feel needs to be put right. Alternatively, we might need some encouragement to bring our purpose to the surface. Our purpose can reveal itself to us in school, at work, in the home, on the sports field, in a caring setting or when we're contemplating our futures. The point is, purpose, our sense of self and our happiness are all interconnected, so what if we could support young people in gaining experience in many different fields so that they may have as many chances as possible to discover their calling, their talent and their passion?

What if we create the circumstances in which we support young people to have the self-awareness, ambition and readiness to take the baton when it's handed to them, wherever and whenever that happens? Engineering random opportunities to explore and creating positive habits of self-reflection and the confidence to take the chance on something new is what this book, and the ideas contained in it, is all about.

The careers context

The careers context recognises that the influences on a person at any time are varied and changeable. I'm a director at NCW community interest company (CIC) and the mission we've created is:

> We believe in the power of careers education, information, advice and guidance (CEIAG) as a driver for change within society, improving life choices and empowering people to take control of their own future.

Nick Newman – founder and CEO of NCW – saw that, after years of inconsistent funding and being marginalised as the poor relation within UK schools, careers education had become confined to having an ever-decreasing influence. Nick decided to act and, in 2011, created the first 'ground-up' movement and celebration of school careers activities, NCW, which evolved from his Twitter campaign #SaveCareers. 'Careers had become a patchwork service across the UK – a postcode lottery dependant on a few good careers folk that would fight to keep it on schools' radars.'

Nick says that since 2018 there has been a renaissance for careers education, which has at last been recognised for its importance in students' transition from education to the world of work, helped by the introduction of the Gatsby Benchmarks and Ofsted's extended remit to report on how schools perform against them. He continues:

At the end of the day this is the one time we shouldn't need the 'why?' question when it comes to quality careers education for young people across the UK: our future success as a nation depends on future generations of young people successfully entering the world of work. Without quality careers guidance, the UK will not be able to prepare them, educate them, ensure they are utilising their skills, make sure their future well-being is maximised by making well-informed decisions – NCW is a grassroots organisation helping those that need it the most! Let's all work together and create more opportunities for young people to see, recognise and experience the future.

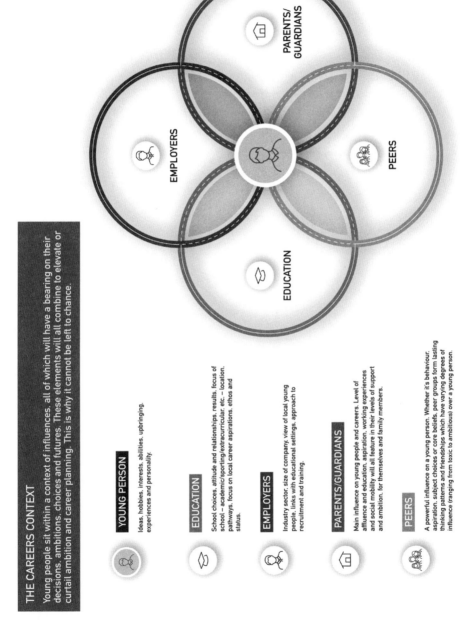

THE CAREERS CONTEXT

Young people sit within a context of influences, all of which will have a bearing on their decisions, ambitions, choices and futures. These elements will all combine to elevate or curtail ambition and career planning. This is why it cannot be left to chance.

YOUNG PERSON

Ideas, hobbies, interests, abilities, upbringing, experiences and personality.

EDUCATION

School choices, attitude and relationships, results, focus of school – academic/sporting/extracurricular, etc. – location, pathways, focus on local career aspirations, ethos and status.

EMPLOYERS

Industry sector, size of company, view of local young people, links with educational settings, approach to recruitment and training.

PARENTS/GUARDIANS

Main influence on young people and careers. Level of affluence and education, aspiration, working experiences and social mobility will all feature in their levels of support and ambition, for themselves and family members.

PEERS

A powerful influence on a young person. Whether it's behaviour, aspiration, subject choices or core beliefs, peer groups form lasting thinking patterns and friendships which have varying degrees of influence (ranging from toxic to ambitious) over a young person.

This book takes this background and position on CEIAG and supports all schools and teachers to embed it into the culture and ethos of the school, into subjects and into extracurricular activities. It also aims to encourage teachers to inspire employers from all industries to support their local schools, colleges and universities to make learning about the future of work and enterprise fun, engaging and informative. There is something for everyone in here and I hope it is of use in your daily practice.

In careers education – as with learning and shoes – there isn't one size to fit all. This is my humble attempt to share what I've learned, to share others' skills and knowledge, and to recruit people who care about our young people to do all we can to support them by creating opportunities for them to shine.

Chapter 2

THE CONTINUUM FOR THE ACQUISITION OF SKILLS AND KNOWLEDGE (CASK)

Life's most persistent and urgent question is, what are you doing for others?

Martin Luther King Jr[1]

Growing up in the UK and being told to 'stop showing off' or 'don't be a bighead' all your life isn't ideal training for the type of high-kicking, jazz-hands, ta-dah, LOOK AT ME skills you will need when writing positively about yourself in applications or expressing yourself in interviews. Suddenly at 16 we need to be confident in describing our skills, talents and aspirations, our positive traits and habits, how we learned them, how we apply them and also what our future is going to look like. In detail. Most adults struggle to declare what we're good at and why we're proud of ourselves.

The learning and skills elements of our lives can be artificially separated during our education, or certainly these elements are scored, recorded and valued differently. It is *essential* that young people's learning *and* skills are valued (and recorded and discussed regularly) as they look ahead at their future career because *both* sets of achievements are brought into play in any job role.

As well as it being important for young people themselves to recognise and record their skills, employers also want to see skills alongside qualifications, which they see as a way of assessing the minimum level of subject knowledge. Of the employers surveyed by BMG Research in September 2013, 79% consider GCSE results to be important, with one-in-four (24%) considering them very useful.[2] In addition, respondents are quoted as saying that they 'look for communication skills, presentation skills and evidence of commitment or reliability through previous jobs or voluntary work' and that it may be

---

1   Martin Luther King Jr, *Strength to Love* (New York: Harper & Row, 1963), p. 72.
2   BMG Research, *New GCSE Grades Research Amongst Employers* [research report prepared for Ofqual] (November 2013), p. 5. Available at: https://assets.publishing. service.gov.uk/government/uploads/system/uploads/attachment_data/file/529390/2013-11-01-bmg-research-with-employers-on-new-gcse-grades.pdf.

'more effective to look at the skills the individual students need to be armed with when they come into the workplace and ensure these are covered'.[3] This is echoed by Linda Emery, head of graduate recruitment at KPMG UK:

When assessing a candidate at graduate level we focus on the capabilities and behaviours that the individual demonstrates, as well as the qualifications they have attained: GCSEs are just one element of this process.[4]

According to research conducted by the Sutton Trust, 'We need to find ways to ensure that all students gain the ability to present themselves well in interview, and to compete with those from more privileged backgrounds.'[5] Founder and chairman of the Sutton Trust Peter Lampl says:

One of the ways in which confidence, aspirations and social skills may provide a career advantage are through their relationship to employability skills and interview performance. Schools and universities should have programmes in place to encourage the development of these skills.[6]

It's worth noting that only 31% of employers surveyed by the British Chambers of Commerce believe that schools are very effective or fairly effective at preparing young people for work,[7] whilst – without a hint of irony – 52% of businesses say that they don't work with schools to offer work-experience placements.[8] Reasons included 'cost and time', 'too much school administration' (is that real or perceived?) and 'a lack of information'.[9]

3   BMG Research, *New GCSE Grades Research Amongst Employers*, p. 7, p. 11.
4   Quoted in Flora Carr, The New GCSE Grades: An Employer's Perspective, *Daily Telegraph* (23 August 2017). Available at: https://www.telegraph.co.uk/education/0/new-gcse-grades-employers-perspective/.
5   Robert de Vries and Jason Rentfrow, *A Winning Personality: The Effects of Background on Personality and Earnings* (London: The Sutton Trust, 2016), p. 1. Available at: https://www.suttontrust.com/wp-content/uploads/2019/12/Winning-Personality-FINAL-1.pdf.
6   de Vries and Rentfrow, *A Winning Personality*, p. 4.
7   British Chambers of Commerce, BCC: Businesses and schools 'still worlds apart' on readiness for work [press release] (11 November 2015). Available at: https://www.britishchambers.org.uk/news/2015/11/bcc-businesses-and-schools-still-worlds-apart-on-readiness-for-work.
8   Cited in Ofsted, *Getting Ready for Work*, p. 14.
9   Ofsted, *Getting Ready for Work*, p. 14.

The continuum for the acquisition of skills and knowledge (CASK) is a set of simple tools which can be used by educators and learners alike to plot learning and skills development on a regular basis as a 'live CV' – a repository and reminder of all the activities undertaken and achievements won to support job applications and answers to questions in interviews. Put another way, the CASK helps young people develop 'informed confidence' and the ability to reflect positively on themselves.

Self-reflection task

List 10 to 15 of your accomplishments *outside* of formal education. (Don't worry if you struggle here,[10] it can be hard and that's why I include a tool to help later on.)

This is a great one to play with your students in form time or with your friends in the office, staffroom or pub. (Handy hint: it's often our friends, family or colleagues who can point out our skills better that we can.)

We find it difficult to answer interview or assessment questions like the awfully unfair 'tell me about yourself', or the more nuanced and direct 'tell me when you worked well as part of a team' or 'how have you used creativity recently?' The CASK helps us to remember our skills, how we acquired them, and how we can show how we've used them positively.

Habits, once learned, will be recited as easily as well-loved song lyrics. This is why it's *crucial* to develop positive self-reflective habits which highlight our skills and abilities – not just our grades. The tools that link to the CASK are all aspects of habit management. Habits can develop without our awareness; they sneak into our daily routines without us noticing most of the time. By focusing on the positive, life-enhancing habits we want our students to develop, we can help them to set themselves up for futures with wider choices, or choices

---

10 If you struggle with this task as an adult, imagine how hard it would have been as a teenager and how hard some of your students would find it.

which are conscious, rather than accidental. The CASK is a method of developing habits to encourage self-reflection, pride, knowledge of self and skills, and a growing awareness of how these skills and habits can be of use in the future.

'You are more than your grades' is a crucial statement for students to take on board in the data-obsessed push to measure everything about school life and performance.

'You are more than your grades' is a powerful statement to remember for teachers, lecturers, mentors and employers when teaching, supporting or appraising people (the young and the not-so-young) in their sphere of influence.

'You are more than your grades' is a powerful reminder for students, parents, teachers, employers and mentors that different people shine in different areas at different times.

Ask yourself:

- Who hasn't made a mistake?
- Who hasn't failed an exam?
- Who hasn't been in trouble in some way?
- Who hasn't been underprepared for a meeting or interview?
- Who hasn't felt stressed, tired, overwhelmed, angry, upset or just plain fed up?

This is why grades aren't everything.

'Careers education is about looking at the young person and not seeing them for what they are now, but seeing them for what they can become', as Emma Hardy – MP for Kingston upon Hull West and Hessle, and Shadow Further Education and Higher Education Minister from 2020 – said, speaking at the launch event for NCW 2019.[11]

The CASK allows the individual and whoever is interrogating/supporting them to remind themselves of their skills and abilities. The CASK reveals the whole person, not just their grades. I see the CASK, alongside academic and personal skills, as the underpinning framework to support what young people can become (see pages 28–29).

---

11 Quoted in National Careers Week, NCW Highlight Report (2019), p. 26. Available at: https://nationalcareersweek.com/download/16707/.

The following table outlines some of the purposes and benefits of the resources (by way of example – it isn't exhaustive).

CASK tool	When to use	Purpose	Benefit
Who Can I Help?	Primary onwards.	Self-reflection and future plans.	Helps students see skills and personal traits.
STAR Model	Late primary, secondary onwards.	Self-reflection and skill expression.	Allows skills to be recognised and communicated easily.
7 Skills Assessment Sheet (7SAS)	Late primary, secondary onwards.	Self-reflection and skill development.	Highlights skills and how to increase/ develop/ express them.
GROW Model	Late primary, secondary onwards.	Personal reflection and goal setting.	Self-set targets are more powerful.
My Crest	Late primary, secondary onwards, transition days.	Personal reflection on values and likes.	Self-awareness and reflection.
Wheel of Life	Primary, secondary onwards.	Reflection on overall happiness levels.	Develops the ability to assess and improve happiness.
Ideal Me	Late primary, secondary onwards, transition days.	Expressing personal aims and targets for the future.	Removing the mystery and starting to envision your own future.

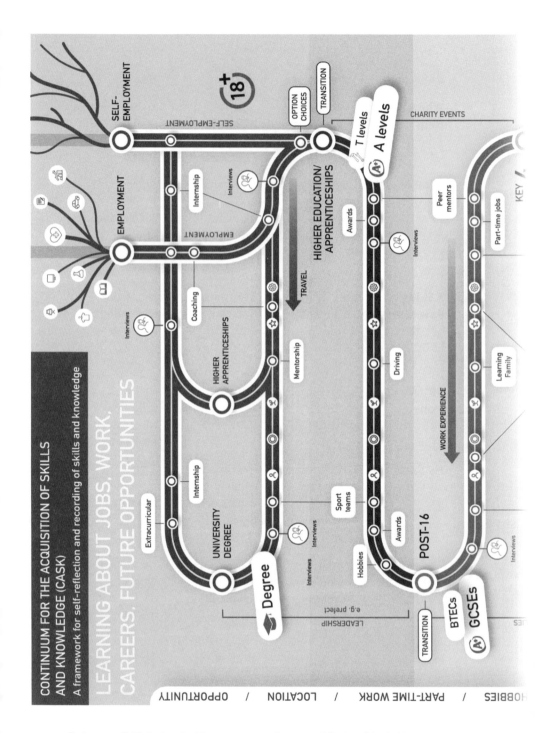

Tools are available to download from: www.crownhouse.co.uk/featured/the-ladder

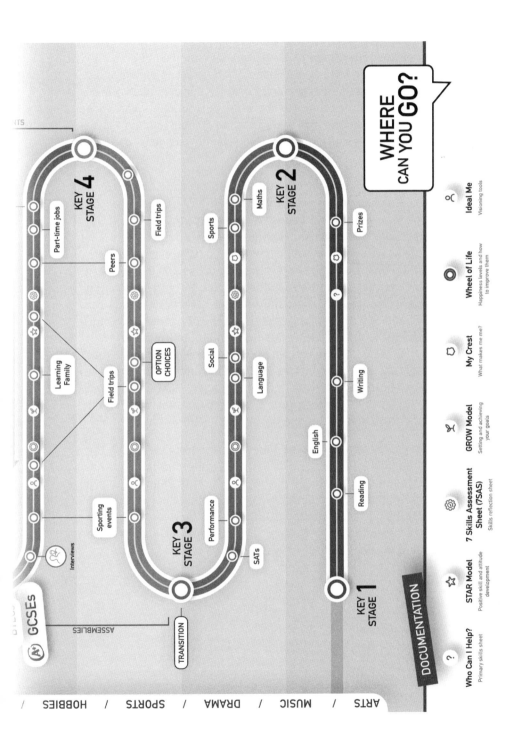

We learn skills and knowledge throughout our lives. The CASK shows the process and this visual can be used as a poster, a personal guide and a tool for planning students' self-development. It's not prescriptive; rather, it is to be used as a basis for you to start engaging young people in learning about themselves. Bring in your own tools alongside it at different times and explore what your students can cope with. You can also use the CASK as a great way to highlight how local and national businesses, charities and other partners can get involved.

The signposts along the way in the CASK represent additional learning and skill opportunities that may not always be perceived as activities or experiences that young people will deem important. All of us have skills and capabilities which we take for granted. For example, if, in workshop introductions, I ask, 'Who's good at languages?', I'll receive a smattering of hands up. Changing the question to 'Who speaks more than one language?', I'll get – depending on where I am in the country – around half the audience's hands up. 'Who speaks more than two languages?': a third of hands remain up; 'Who speaks more than three languages?' and there's often still half a dozen hands in the air. The tools in the CASK allow you to guide your students to reflect on themselves broadly and begin to appreciate their talents. Speaking three or more languages, for example, will have huge implications for their future, opening up careers with multilingual and travel aspects to them.

When linked to the careers context Venn diagram from Chapter 1, the CASK will highlight to the student that they have choices and that *their* decisiveness is important – with the support of different people at different phases. Choice develops responsibility. Choice develops agency. Choice develops confidence. All of the downloadable tools can be used by students of any age or ability – as an educator please use your skill in adapting and applying them as is appropriate.[12]

---

12 Tools are available to download from: www.crownhouse.co.uk/featured/the-ladder

Self-reflection task

Before you give these resources to your students or recommend them to others, please take some time to use them yourself. Have a go: allow the tools to get your grey-matter working, get another perspective on yourself, consider how you've grown throughout your life and see where the elements of the CASK have been strongest for you – during primary or secondary education or HE, work, self-employment, extracurricular activities, sports, hobbies, etc.

When you've completed the tasks, share your responses with a partner, colleagues, friends, family members, etc. and talk about them. Everyone has experienced different learning at different times in their lives, and reflecting on this with others can be very illuminating.

The CASK tools

Who Can I Help?

From the start of school, children are allowed to explore creativity, exercise, social activity, reading and writing, as well as other project-based learning. These all develop skills which we can record in an age-appropriate way. I developed the Who Can I Help? tool for NCW to enable younger or less-able pupils to identify and record their skills and qualities, and to see how they could be put to good use in society. It deliberately does *not* ask 'what job do you want to do?' because this will narrow children's views of careers and work; rather, I wanted to encourage self-awareness and pride in themselves and their skills.

WHO CAN I HELP?

Primary Resources

Name: _____ Class: _____

Who will I help? _____

What will I do? _____

The 7 Skills We Need

Do I have these skills? Score yourself out of ten for each skill.

1. Great ideas ○
2. Good at using information ○
3. Being adaptable to change ○
4. Being good in a team or a good team leader ○
5. Being a great communicator ○
6. Being a problem solver ○
7. Being curious and imaginative ○

Personal Qualities

Do I have these qualities?

1. Bravery ○
2. Friendliness ○
3. Helpfulness ○
4. Kindness ○
5. Decisiveness ○
6. _____ ○
7. _____ ○
8. _____ ○

National Careers Week

NCW

More resources are available at nationalcareersweek.com

Tools are available to download from: www.crownhouse.co.uk/featured/the-ladder
This resource is from a wide selection available at: https://ncw2020.co.uk/.

7 Skills Assessment Sheet (7SAS)

This tool allows teachers to actively develop students' confidence and awareness of their skills, where they will become useful and how to write and talk about them. Too many students are dismissed (or may feel that they are) because they can't see themselves in a particular career in the future. The CASK tools are about increasing young people's awareness of their social capital, skills and their own agency. The 7SAS supports self-reflection and allows students to link who they are to what they are learning and how this will be relevant to their future lives and careers (see page 35).

It is based on Dr Tony Wagner's list of seven essential skills, which he compiled from his research into achievement:

- **Critical Thinking and Problem Solving**
- **Collaboration Across Networks and Leading by Influence**
- **Agility and Adaptability**
- **Initiative and Entrepreneurialism**
- **Effective Oral and Written Communication**
- **Accessing and Analyzing Information**
- **Curiosity and Imagination** [13]

You might notice that the Who Can I Help? sheet also addresses these skills – modified and presented in age-appropriate language. It's not just in school that we see the seven skills in evidence: we develop and demonstrate them during sport, work experience, part-time work, volunteering, extended learning activities, mentoring, at home, and in our hobbies and interests. If employers want to see curiosity and imagination and your students haven't been cataloguing, valuing or even noticing it in themselves, then they're not going to be able to readily offer examples in an application, personal statement, CV or interview.

The 7SAS helps people (not just young people!) to assess and rank their skills on a regular basis. We need to develop the habit of reflecting on our skills and being able to speak positively about them when

---

13 Wagner, *The Global Achievement Gap*, p. 67.

asked. This takes practice before it becomes habit, so it's important to start early. As the child makes progress throughout their schooling, it is worth starting to build the skills of reflection and self-awareness (and therefore confidence) year by year. The aim is not to get high scores across the board, but to see where our strengths lie and where we can improve over time. The 7SAS asks the student to record the date and thus allows a longitudinal vision of development over time: the self-reflection scores are essential to ownership, as are the questions about where the skills and competencies have been demonstrated.

An alternative and less-threatening way to introduce the 7SAS may be to ask students to team up and consider how their friends use the skills and attributes. Often, an objective viewpoint from a friend, classmate or colleague can provide more insight (and likely higher scores) than self-assessment can. However, the 7SAS is intended as a valuable reflection tool which puts the power of assessment into the hands of the person completing it. It is important that students can eventually learn to harness this powerful element of self-advocacy. Supporting self-reflection, rather than performing the assessment of them, is really important in terms of students taking ownership of – and taking ownership of improving – their own skills and abilities. Being an active participant in your own development is an empowering and crucial step up the ladder of success.

As Warren Johnson, head of PR agency W Communication, says about many of the young people who could be applying for their WX internship programme, 'They already have those in-built skills – even if they don't realise it – that clients and brands are looking for.'[14] The good news is that the 7SAS will support young people to become more familiar with their personal qualities, which, in turn, will inform their career aspirations, focus and achievements.

---

14 Arvind Hickman, W Launches Social Enterprise to Fundamentally Change Industry's Talent Pipeline, PR Week (24 October 2019). Available at: https://www.prweek.com/article/1663527/w-launches-social-enterprise-fundamentally-change-industrys-talent-pipeline.

7 Skills Assessment Sheet (7SAS)

Student Name _____

Form Group _____   Date _____

Key Skill	Recognised it today	Used it today	Improved a little			Improved to some extent				Improved considerably			How can I prove this? How could I improve this?
Critical thinking and problem solving			1	2	3	4	5	6	7	8	9	10	
Collaboration and leading by influence			1	2	3	4	5	6	7	8	9	10	
Agility and adaptability			1	2	3	4	5	6	7	8	9	10	
Initiative and entrepreneurialism			1	2	3	4	5	6	7	8	9	10	
Effective oral and written communication			1	2	3	4	5	6	7	8	9	10	
Accessing and analysing information			1	2	3	4	5	6	7	8	9	10	
Curiosity and imagination			1	2	3	4	5	6	7	8	9	10	

Tools are available to download from: www.crownhouse.co.uk/featured/the-ladder

The 7SAS can also help to develop thinking which opposes standard-ised stereotypes – 'boys are lazy' and 'girls are bossy', for example. As Sheryl Sandberg, chief operating officer of Facebook and author of *Lean In*,[15] says of her Ban Bossy campaign: 'we call girls bossy on the playground [...] We call them too aggressive or other B-words in the workplace.'[16] By using the 7SAS as a reflective document, we can open up discussions about what these behaviours look like and the language often used which perpetuates the gender divide.

Using the 7SAS regularly will permit the user to recall incidents in which they used specific skills and record and reflect on them whilst they are still fresh in the mind. This will serve 7SAS users well as a habit. The most important element of the 7SAS habit is to learn to understand and convey your own skills: firstly, to yourself to reinforce your self-belief and confidence, and, secondly, to others in written or verbal form.

Teachers can use the 7SAS to draw attention to and explore different focus points:

- Which jobs use this skill?
- How would this skill support others?
- Outside of school/work, where else will this skill be useful?
- Which skills are you going to focus on developing and using in the next term/year?
- How could you develop skill A, B or C so you would be better prepared for job X, Y or Z?
- Why do you think this mix of seven skills will be so useful in the future?
- Which of the skills are most/least crucial?
- How would you rank the skills?
- How would you represent your own skill mix?

---

15 Sheryl Sandberg, *Lean In: Women, Work and the Will to Lead* (London: WH Allen, 2013).
16 Quoted in Cynthia McFadden and Jake Whitman, Sheryl Sandberg Launches 'Ban Bossy' Campaign to Empower Girls to Lead, *ABC News* (10 March 2014). Available at: https://abcnews.go.com/US/sheryl-sandberg-launches-ban-bossy-campaign-empower-girls/story?id=22819181.

Ideal Me

During school – and especially at transition times between primary and secondary school or secondary school and sixth form and beyond – Ideal Me can be a valuable tool. Ideal Me allows students the opportunity to complete the sheet in whatever way they wish – drawing, colouring, sticky notes, collage, writing, etc. It's a vision of the future which invites consideration of the whole person, not just academic successes but also their cultural, career and lifestyle aspirations. During transitions between school settings, Ideal Me facilitates discussion with individual students, allowing teachers to get to know their interests and a bit more about their personalities. Children's drawings can also contain clues to fears and stresses, so can reveal pastoral needs which may need to be supported. It's a simple and less-threatening way to get students to reflect on where they are and to project forwards.

Ideal Me can also help teams to get to know one another: it could be a good way to get to know new colleagues during INSET sessions or for getting disparate groups of people to communicate as an ice-breaker at the start of a new term. Ideal Me is included in the CASK tools as a flexible device for people of all ages to use in any number of ways to promote self-reflection and future visioning (see page 38).

My Crest

My Crest is another simple and effective tool which allows younger pupils – and those with special educational needs and disabilities (SEND) or English as an additional language (EAL) – to express themselves in pictures rather than words. It allows the exploration of elements of character which some might find difficult to express in writing but more straightforward in pictures. As with the majority of the tools in the CASK, My Crest can be revisited a number of times: as a child's circumstances change or if they experience growth or stress. It can even be used by older students and staff. Being shield-shaped it may also connote the idea of being a superhero, with superpowers such as resilience, kindness, strength, bravery, etc (see page 39).

IDEAL ME

Use this Ideal Me resource to imagine yourself in the future – you could draw an outline of you, design yourself as a superhero, use collage, draw a picture of what you're going to look like surrounded by the things you love ... Just imagine the future you that you want to create for yourself.

NAME:

AGE:

THIS IS ME IN

_____ YEARS

Complete with pen, pencil, collage, colours, sticky notes ...

BE **BOLD**

THINK ABOUT YOUR:

- LIFE
- FRIENDS
- HOBBIES
- LEARNING
- WORK
- HOME
- HOLIDAYS
- LEGACY

Tools are available to download from: www.crownhouse.co.uk/featured/the-ladder

My Crest

Design your own crest. Think about what you like doing and how you like to spend your time. Then, think about what this could mean for your future career – what could you do when you leave school, college or university?

Tools are available to download from: www.crownhouse.co.uk/featured/the-ladder

The Wheel of Life

The Wheel of Life is a well-established coaching tool which is credited to Paul Meyer and has been used as a metaphor for balance and teaching about lifestyle choices. A version of it is supposed to have been used by Buddha to teach his disciples about enlightenment and the pathways thereto. The two simplified versions of the Wheel of Life presented and utilised in the CASK (one for primary and one for secondary) will allow anyone to assess their current levels of happiness in different areas of their life.

The Wheel of Life can be adapted if you think that would be useful, but I have found that the following areas are most relevant to young people:

- Relationships – friends, family, teachers, boyfriends, girlfriends, etc.
- School, work or career plans – grades, peers, long-term vision, achievements.
- Health and fitness – how you look after yourself, your eating and exercise habits.
- Skills – how good you are at picking up new things such as interpersonal skills, cooking, sports, creative crafts, driving, etc.
- Use of time – we all have 24 hours a day, how good are you at using them?
- Hobbies and interests – what are yours? Do you make time for them? Are they helpful and positive?

Primary Wheel of Life

The primary Wheel of Life could be used as a way of assessing how the child is feeling on a given day. It could potentially highlight areas of unhappiness/worry/discomfort and open up lines of discussion which should be sensitively handled by staff. Because the wheel touches on familial and personal relationships as well as school-based friendships, care should be used by teachers when discussing issues in class, as low scores may bring to light significant unhappiness or challenges in a child's life. If used during transitions between primary and secondary school, it can be a valuable tool to see if there has been any change in students' outlooks.

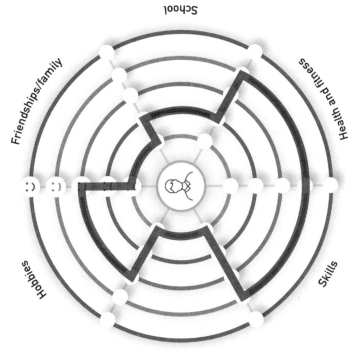

WHEEL OF LIFE   PRIMARY

School choices, attitude and relationships, results, focus of school – academic/ sporting/extracurricular, etc. – location, pathways, focus on career aspirations, ethos and status.

:) Great

:) Good

:| OK

:(Bad

:(Awful

Tools are available to download from: www.crownhouse.co.uk/featured/the-ladder

41

Secondary and above Wheel of Life

Your completed Wheel of Life gives you a simple visual representation of how happy you are with the life you have now. It therefore tells you what *you* need to focus on to make it better/more balanced/happier. Students can review theirs and then *decide* what to do with regard to the lowest scoring sections to make them feel happier. Start with the lowest-scoring one or two sections and see what could be done to improve them incrementally. Suggest to the students that they shouldn't be tempted to try to jump from a 2 to a 5 in one go, but plan and take it gradually and get some support from someone who knows and cares for them – a parent, teacher, friend – and ask for their honest feedback. One of the most powerful elements of the Wheel of Life is that the picture you see is the picture *you* created. The scores are yours, so you own them.

Wheels work best when they are balanced – when they aren't, they wobble or stop working – so the idea is to try and bring low scores up to meet the higher ones. Each section needs to be considered and some realistic plans for change put in place. The GROW Model which follows offers ideas for making changes that stick (see page 47).

As a worked example (see page 44): a 13-year-old student has low scores for relationships/family; use of time; and school, work or career plans, but why? After a two-minute chat, you learn that they spend five to six hours a day on their games console and are often too tired or distracted to do their homework, which in turn gives them low scores on tests and low effort grades, which upsets their parents, creating a vicious cycle.

As another example, the scores for the 15-year-old student profiled on page 45 could indicate that the student is worried about their exams and is so focused on revision that everything else is suffering. Life should be balanced – hence the wheel!

Use of time is a common low-scoring area for young people. Ask a roomful of 13-, 14- and 15-year-olds if they have 'use of time' as their lowest, or one of the lowest, scoring sections and two-thirds of hands go up. It's not always social media and watching on-demand TV, but quite often it is. This is a valuable insight for teachers, parents and, most crucially, the students themselves. Seeing their habits laid out in front of them, according to their own assessment of how happy they are with them, is a powerful agent for change if we invite them to take charge of the picture of their lives. Reflecting, visualising, deciding and committing: these are all essential behaviours of a well-rounded individual. A person who is willing to take charge of their own thoughts, feelings and behaviours is on their way to becoming more assertive and ambitious, because they understand that they are the captain of their own voyage.

The Wheel of Life again comes with a safety caveat – this tool does open up the possibility of discussion of a personal nature which students might not normally enter into in school. You will know your students, but caution needs to be taken when opening up debates about their personal lives and happiness. Signs of distress and non-completion should be handled sensitively and possibly passed to pastoral staff. We need to ensure that they get the support they need if they disclose a problem that they are having at home or a mental health issue, for example.

WHEEL OF LIFE SECONDARY AND ABOVE

School choices, attitude and relationships, results, focus of school – academic/ sporting/extracurricular, etc. – location, pathways, focus on career aspirations, ethos and status.

5 Great

4 Good

3 OK

2 Bad

1 Awful

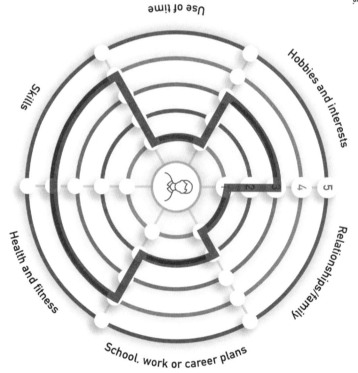

Use of time

Hobbies and interests

Skills

Relationships/family

Health and fitness

School, work or career plans

13-YEAR-OLD

15-YEAR-OLD

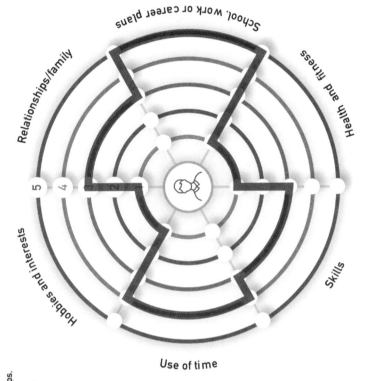

School, work or career plans

Health and fitness

Skills

Use of time

Hobbies and interests

Relationships/family

Relationships/family

5 4 3 2 1

WHEEL OF LIFE   SECONDARY AND ABOVE

School choices, attitude and relationships, results, focus of school – academic/ sporting/extracurricular, etc. – location, pathways, focus on career aspirations, ethos and status.

5 Great
4 Good
3 OK
2 Bad
1 Awful

The GROW Model

Goal setting is crucial to the development of your future.

Without goals we have nowhere to aim – how would a top striker, business person or astronaut cope if they had no goals to aim for?!

Goal
What specifically are you aiming for?

Reality
Is it really possible?

Options
What ways are there to get to where you want to be?

Will
What will you do from today, to make this happen?

The GROW Model

The GROW Model allows aspiration to become a set of realistic steps towards a goal. GROW is an established coaching tool which was first published in 1992 in John Whitmore in his *Coaching for Performance* book.[17] It has since been adapted and amended and used for sports coaching, in business as well as in family therapy books.

GROW is a simple four-stage model which can be used in conjunction with the Wheel of Life to think about behaviour change strategies. It helps young people to become more focused on their future selves and also to develop a positive vision of the journey they will take to get there. It's also a handy reflection tool to use on a termly basis to refocus energy and attention. Once someone has looked objectively at their situation and identified which elements of their lives *they* are happy or unhappy with, the GROW Model will help them to take action to improve their lives, achieve their dreams and overcome challenges in their day-to-day lives.

The two most important elements of the GROW Model are setting the goal in the first place and committing to actions; however, each step is important in this process.

Goals need to be specific and tightly bounded in terms of time and destination, otherwise how will you know when you've met the goal?

Reality doesn't invite just a yes-or-no answer, it gives you the chance to reflect on the goal and how achievable it is. For example, if you wanted to be 6 foot 2 inches tall and you're 5 foot 6 inches, this isn't something you can realistically aspire to. If you wanted to learn to ride a motorbike before you are 18 or to start a business selling cakes by the time you're 21 then you *could* do this.

Options are the *ways* in which you could achieve your goals. So if you decide you want to learn to ride a motorbike before you're 18, then you could find a training school, save up to buy a small motorbike, borrow one from your parents or use one from the training school until you pass your test. These are the possibilities. Once one is chosen, then getting finance, asking your family for a loan, or saving up from your part-time job are

---

17 John Whitmore, *Coaching for Performance: A Practical Guide to Growing Your Own Skills* (London: Nicholas Brealey Publishing, 1992), p. 173.

the next possible steps. Booking lessons and a test would also be part of the options.

Will needs to be expressed as something which you commit to doing. So if you want to improve your grades, then increasing your concentration and asking friends/parents/coaches/tutors/mentors for support and advice must be steps to take. You need to show commitment and share your aspiration publicly so other people can help hold you to account.

When used in conjunction with the Wheel of Life, the GROW Model will allow young people (and potentially school staff and, indeed, all adults) to reflect on their situation and take action in areas of their lives which could be happier.

Not all students will want to or be able to access the learning in these tools when first offered. As getting to grips with feelings, happiness and taking control of our own destiny is a long journey, the earlier and more frequently this opportunity is offered, the easier it is to take it up and ideally make it into a positive habit. Luckily, there is a simple tool we can use to build the habit and skill of self-reflection: the STAR Model.

The STAR Model

What happens when someone is asked to highlight their skills, abilities and experiences?

'Er, well, um, let me think, oh, now ...'

See? It's difficult to do, isn't it? That's why the STAR Model is so helpful.

The STAR Model is a well-established method for giving feedback at work – during appraisals, in performance management reviews and in assessing how well a project has been delivered. For our purposes, it will be applied as a tool for helping students to evidence their skill-set and highlight how they have been able to successfully use their skills and attributes, or, if they were unsuccessful in a given task, how they have shown/plan to show improvement (see page 51).

The STAR Model is as follows:

Situation – where were you being asked to use these skills or attributes?

Task – what were you personally doing or being asked to do?

Action – explain what exactly you did in this context.

Result – what were the specific outcomes of this activity and what were the learning experiences for you personally?

This tool is superb for a number of reasons. It can:

- Help to form the positive habit of self-reflection.
- Encourage self-reflection so students can develop examples of their skills in practice.
- Support applications for work experience.
- Support applications for jobs/apprenticeships/internships.
- Support applications for university/college.
- Support interviews by providing a scaffold of examples to use in answers.
- Allow analysis of skills against job or course specifications and outlines.
- Facilitate reflection on personal achievements.
- Be combined with the 7SAS to see which skills have been used and where.
- Highlight areas for improvement across the 7SAS areas.
- Develop students' confidence in their skills and awareness of their abilities.

Examples of the STAR Model can be used to develop thinking about skills and achievements before interviews and when writing applications. Short stories of achievement can be more compelling (and more interesting to read) than a list of qualities and abilities. Here are a couple of examples:

Leadership: Once, my hockey team were playing in a tournament and had reached the semi-final (situation). I pulled a leg muscle when we were already 2–1 down. As I'm a midfielder and the captain (task), the role is crucial, so I decided (action) to substitute myself for a fitter player and we won the game (result).

Creativity: As part of an enterprise competition (situation), my team were delivering a presentation (task) and we wanted to stand out. As two of the four team members are in the choir, we decided to write and perform (action) a jingle to back up our new business idea. None of the other teams took this approach and the judges loved it – we were one of the winning teams (result).

When preparing for an interview, I often advise the people I coach to have a few 'back pocket' answers prepared. The STAR Model makes this easier and provides a structure to ensure answers are succinct and to the point. This tool can also be used for remembering different aspects of our endeavours for applications or simply to use in conversations with friends, peers, colleagues or employers. In this way, it also enables people who may be shy or lacking in self-confidence to prepare themselves for interactions in which they need to talk about their qualities.

The STAR Model

What are you a star at?

Think of everything you've achieved in all aspects of your life – sports, hobbies, home, family, work – and present them as little stories using the STAR Model. This is a great way to see our skills and be able to tell people about them in applications and interviews. Start the habit, get your story straight!

Situation Where were you?			
Task What was your role?			
Actions What did you do?			
Results What was the outcome?			

Conclusion

The CASK is an evolving framework which is intended as a starting point for each establishment to add to as required. The tools in this chapter will be available on this book's website and via Innovative Enterprise.[18] The tools will overlap at times. They will be useful for specific tasks at particular ages and stages, and can be used as bridging tools to enable students to link their studies and pastimes with their futures. They are deliberately flexible and can be developed and added to by teachers to help get the best from their students and to support them to develop and reflect on their skills.

Why not try using some of them in an INSET session to get to know your colleagues a little bit better or as self-reflection exercises?

A note on CVs and applications

This book deliberately doesn't offer tools to support students to create a curriculum vitae (CV). There are myriad online support tools for this and pretty much every online careers management system for schools will have a CV section.

The work you do with students using the tools in this book will create great habits, effective self-reflection, better self-awareness and more succinct ways of expressing skills and abilities and revealing the person *behind* the grades.

Other support for CV development comes from initiatives like Barclays LifeSkills, national programmes of support and local CEIAG and business support provision through Local Enterprise Partnerships (LEPs)[19]and your local Careers Hubs.[20]

CVs are still a valid and enduring part of the career journey; however, the way CVs are devised and used is changing, and innovations in

---

18 See www.innovativeenterprise.co.uk.
19 LEPs exist in each UK nation to support businesses locally. England: https://www.lepnetwork.net/; Scotland: https://education.gov.scot/improvement/self-evaluation/education-employer-partnerships/; Wales: https://careerswales.gov.wales/employers/working-with-schools.
20 A Careers Hub is a collection of 20–40 schools who collaborate to deliver partnership progress towards supporting student futures. Information available at: https://www.careersandenterprise.co.uk/about-us/our-network/careers-hubs.

technology have led to new and exciting ways to highlight skills, experiences and ambitions:

- Infographic/pictorial CVs (great for creative people).
- Video CVs.
- Online CV systems.
- Personal websites.
- globalbridge profiles (self-curated social-media-friendly secure online CV).
- LinkedIn profiles (for over 18s).
- Online profiles on Monster Jobs, Indeed and other recruitment/ work brokerage systems.
- Personal statements – an essential section on the UCAS application form.

Many factors will determine which CV 'system' you subscribe to: your local partners or the latest industry developments and how relevant they are to your students, for example. CV templates are available from many sources, so please select the best one for your students. There are even YouTube, UCAS[21] and BBC Bitesize Careers[22] tutorials about how to create the perfect CV, application cover letters and personal statements. Remember: curriculum vitae roughly translates from the Latin as 'the course of my life' or 'my life list', but it can and should be so much more than that, as I'm sure you will agree.

In conclusion, the CASK is a grand term for what we learn in life, but I hope the framework I've created and the tools I've applied to it will help to show that we never stop learning. The CASK is a comprehensive, if not exhaustive, way of curating your skills for a variety of uses, chief amongst them being self-realisation and the ability to express yourself in a variety of situations through a variety of media.

The CASK is a tool to develop specific habits which will allow young people to benefit from the random opportunities you encourage them to undertake. Let's hope it's a positive self-fulfilling prophecy.

---

21 See https://www.ucas.com/undergraduate/applying-university/filling-your-ucas-undergraduate-application.
22 See https://www.bbc.co.uk/bitesize/careers.

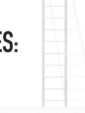

Chapter 3

EQUALITY OF CAREERS OPPORTUNITIES: THE RESEARCH

He [John F. Kennedy] believed that every man can make a difference – and that every man should try.

Jacqueline Kennedy[1]

If you're reading this book, it's likely that you are interested in supporting young people with their future aspirations and career plans. This section highlights research and information about the different needs young people might have, depending on their upbringing, background and circumstances. This section also covers stereotypes and how we should take them into consideration in our activities and work to overcome them.

Stereotypes are everywhere – gender, class, race, physical and mental abilities – all exist and are highlighted by 'traditional' roles and the language we use. Careers are no different. Stereotypes also reinforce inequality. Focusing on one skill area, the Royal Academy of Engineering's 2019 report states that:

There have been welcome increases in the number of people undertaking engineering apprenticeships since 2013, although female and ethnic minority representation are abysmally low, at 6% and 8% respectively.[2]

Without definitive and decisive action to change the narrative around work, jobs and careers, stereotypes and inequalities will persist. When do we need to start talking to young people about careers to

---

1 For a discussion of the source, see: Stacey Flores Chandler, Did JFK Say It?: 'One Person Can Make A Difference and Everyone Should Try', *The JFK Library Archives* [blog] (28 October 2019). Available at: https://jfk.blogs.archives.gov/2019/10/28/make-a-difference-quote/.
2 Royal Academy of Engineering, *Engineering Skills for the Future: The 2013 Perkins Review Revisited* (2019), p. 8. Available at: www.raeng.org.uk/perkins2019.

broaden their ideas about what they could do in future? As early as possible is the answer.

In UK schools, careers education in its broadest sense has (when there's funding and an impetus for it) typically started in the last couple of years before GCSEs, as the students settle into the options they have chosen in Year 9. The rationale for this is, I'm sure, that 'They don't need it until they leave secondary school at 16.' *Wrong*.

Careers advice needs to be:

- Earlier.
- Broader.
- Better.

By the time students have stumbled their way into choosing subjects – a choice often based either on what they like/are good at *or* what they knew they could pass an exam in *or* what they know will help the next stage of their learning or employment journey (or to a lesser extent, what their parents want them to do/what their friends are doing[3]) – it's too late, in many cases, to easily divert from that pathway. They might find then that careers which require alternative GCSEs, or different pathways such as those offered at studio schools or university technical colleges (UTCs), are closed to them – or at least obstructed or delayed.

Stereotyping: it's everyone's problem. Research by UK charity Education and Employers received 20,000 responses from children aged 7–11 who were asked to draw their future careers. The findings suggested that gendered stereotyping exists from 7 years old and:

- **Across the sample, children's aspirations appear to be shaped by gender-specific ideas about certain jobs. Boys overwhelmingly aspire to take on roles in traditionally male dominated sectors and professions.**

- **Gendered patterns also emerge in STEM-related professions. Over four times the number of boys wanted to become Engineers (civil, mechanical, electrical) compared to girls. Moreover, nearly double the number of boys wanted to become scientists**

---

3   Wenchao Jin, Alastair Muriel and Luke Sibieta, *Subject and Course Choices at Ages 14 and 16 Amongst Young People in England: Insights from Behavioural Economics*. Research Report DFE-RR160 (May 2010), p. 25. Available at: https://assets.publishing.service.gov. uk/government/uploads/system/uploads/attachment_data/file/182677/DFE-RR160.pdf.

compared to girls in our sample. However, strikingly, two and half times the number of girls wanted to become Doctors compared to boys, and nearly four times the number of girls want to become Vets compared to boys.[4]

An update to this research was reported by the BBC, as Andreas Schleicher, the Organisation for Economic Co-operation and Development (OECD) director of education and skills, pronounced that '"talent is being wasted" because of ingrained stereotyping about social background, gender and race'.[5] He backed Education and Employers' findings as he spoke at their conference, confirming that 'minimal changes' to attitudes on career aspirations are made between the ages of 7 and 17 and he stated that pupils must be encouraged to keep their options open. One of the most powerful ways is by meeting and hearing from a diverse range of people in a variety of jobs from primary school onwards.

Speaking as if he is a natural advocate for this book, Mr Schleicher went on to say: 'It's a question of social justice and common sense to tackle ingrained assumptions as early as possible or they will be very tough to unpick later on.' I couldn't agree more.

Who you know matters. The *Drawing the Future* researchers also asked the children if they knew anyone who did the jobs they drew. The majority (61.2%) knew no one who did the job; of those who did know someone, 33% had an extended family member who did the job, and 26% had a parent or guardian who did the job.[6] What of those who don't know anyone in that line of work?

What if your school arranges work experience only for pupils whose academic achievements are lower than expected?[7] This was found to be the case in several schools that contributed their views to Ofsted's *Getting Ready for Work* report. School leaders frequently suggested that arranging work experience was time-consuming and impractical (as it used to be centrally organised in each region

---

4   Nick Chambers, Elnaz T. Kashefpakdel, Jordan Rehill and Christian Percy, *Drawing the Future: Exploring the Career Aspirations of Primary School Children from Around the World* (London: Education and Employers, 2018), p. iv. Available at: https://www. educationandemployers.org/wp-content/uploads/2018/01/Drawing-the-Future-FINAL-REPORT.pdf.

5   Sean Coughlan, Careers Ambitions 'Already Limited by Age of Seven', *BBC News* (15 October 2019). Available at: https://www.bbc.co.uk/news/amp/education-50042459.

6   Chambers et al., *Drawing the Future*, p. 29.

7   Ofsted, *Getting Ready for Work*, p. 13.

and is now contracted out at a cost to individual schools).[8] What this may mean is that those students seen as 'below par' academically are being guided/encouraged/forced onto a more 'vocational route', rather than given inspirational experiences which would help to increase focus, aspiration and hopefully academic performance.

What if your school tasks you to arrange your own work experience at 14 or 15? Great if you're a confident, outgoing young person and/or have parents or family members in a variety of organisations and industries, and at a high enough level to influence getting you a place. What if you're not confident, you have a learning difficulty, you have experienced adverse childhood experiences (ACEs),[9] you find it difficult to use the phone or you come from a family with experience of multiple deprivations? Then it's not so good – in fact it's extremely difficult and downright unfair to expect you to arrange the work experience yourself without support.

As the *Getting Ready for Work* report states:

Some of the schools visited required pupils to find their own placements. In one such school, leaders argued that this encouraged 'independence and resilience'. However, while this may be true to a certain extent, it also reinforces advantages for those pupils with parents who have good connections in industry and business.[10]

The converse must therefore also be true: disadvantage is reinforced and perpetuated.

What if you do benefit from work experience at 14 or 15 years old? The *Getting Ready for Work* report states that:

Pupils who had access to quality work experience benefitted from exposure to real life examples of careers. Pupils' next steps and career choices were often refined by the practical experience. [..] For many pupils, these opportunities were valuable because of the

---

8   Ofsted, *Getting Ready for Work*, p. 13.
9   Stressful events during childhood which can affect development, socialising, behaviour and performance. Examples include domestic violence, mental health issues in a parent, divorce or separation of parents, being a victim of neglect or any form of abuse. An excellent summary can be found at http://www.healthscotland.scot/population-groups/children/adverse-childhood-experiences-aces/overview-of-aces.
10 Ofsted, *Getting Ready for Work*, p. 13.

different knowledge and skills they learned to those in the rest of their school lessons:

'Well, I had to be organised and sorted – you do here too, but it doesn't matter that much. But on work experience you feel on your own.'[11]

So, work experience can be a good source of practice in skills such as planning and organisation, and developing independence.

What if you attend a school that is located in one of the cold-spot areas of multiple disadvantage highlighted by the Careers and Enterprise Company? According to the Careers and Enterprise Company, 'The careers Cold Spots use a basket of data to identify which areas of the country are most in need of career support'.[12]

The cold-spots idea uses a temperature guide to the areas where young people and their career aspirations are affected by disadvantages. Any one of these factors measured would be a disadvantage, but, when combined with others, the difficulties likely to be experienced by students in that region are magnified.

Measures of these disadvantages include:

- Deprivation indicators (e.g. percentage of children on free school meals).
- Employer engagement indicators (e.g. availability of work experience and inspiration offers).
- Outcome indicators for young people (e.g. GCSE attainment, STEM A level uptake (overall and girls as a sub-set), numbers of NEETs).

They identified these cold spots in large swathes of England.[13] These areas are represented by the darker areas of the maps that follow. The research enabled prioritisation of targeted activities and funding in each region to 'warm up' the cold spots (to continue their analogy) by specific interventions designed to improve the careers support provided to young people and educational establishments.

---

11 Ofsted, *Getting Ready for Work*, pp. 13–14.
12 Careers and Enterprise Company, *Updating the Careers Cold Spots: The Careers and Enterprise Prioritisation Indicators* (London: Careers and Enterprise Company, 2018), p. iv. Available at: https://www.careersandenterprise.co.uk/sites/default/files/uploaded/updating_the_careers_cold_spots_report.pdf.
13 Careers and Enterprise Company, *Prioritisation Index 2015*, p. 7.

Since the cold-spots report was issued and the Careers and Enterprise Company advocated for using the Gatsby Benchmarks to assess CEIAG performance, there has been progress in varying degrees across the UK. In the Careers and Enterprise Company's *State of The Nation 2019* report it was found that 'All LEPs have made progress on at least some of their benchmarks' and that one of the highest achieving LEPs was Humber[14] (region 18 on these maps), with Lancashire (region 19 on these maps) also showing progress across the time period. We can see the progress over time by comparing the 2015 map (see page 61) with the 2018 update (see page 62).

The updated map highlights fewer darker (colder) spots, a reduced maximum of five rather than six cold spots and areas which show no cold-spot indicators. The map does still show many areas with multiple disadvantages, highlighting the continued need for careers support for young people and there is still a large number of LEP regions with two or more indicators. There is still much work to do.

What if you're a child in one of the areas which still have a number of cold-spot indicators? Areas where you and many of your friends qualify for free school meals, where large-scale employment in traditional heavy industries was decimated and employment levels have dwindled for the past two or three decades, where there aren't enough businesses to offer work experience or inspiration and where a good number of your older peers are NEETs? What examples, role models and variety of future careers are you going to see? Even with the efforts being made, the answer is likely to be *not many*, and what you do see is unlikely to be representative of what's on offer in the big wide world.

What if you're a student from a black and minority ethnic (BAME) background who gets into university and then, even with the same or higher grades, you're 15.6% less likely to attain a first or 2:1 degree than your white counterparts?[15] This is when you need advocates and people who will stand in your corner – even when you don't know you need an advocate in your corner.

Writing in *RIFE: 21 Stories from Britain's Youth*, Ilyas Nagdee speaks passionately about his experience of growing up in Manchester and

---

14 Careers and Enterprise Company, *State of the Nation 2019: Progress Towards the Gatsby Benchmarks in England's Secondary Schools and Colleges in Local Enterprise Partnerships* (2019), p. 1. Available at: https://www.careersandenterprise.co.uk/sites/default/files/uploaded/1273_state_of_the_nation_lep_analysis_2019_final_1019.pdf.
15 See https://ecu.ac.uk/guidance-resources/student-recruitment-retention-attainment/student-attainment/degree-attainment-gaps/.

THE CAREERS & ENTERPRISE COMPANY

Prioritisation indicators: total number of indicators in "bottom third" range identified in each LEP

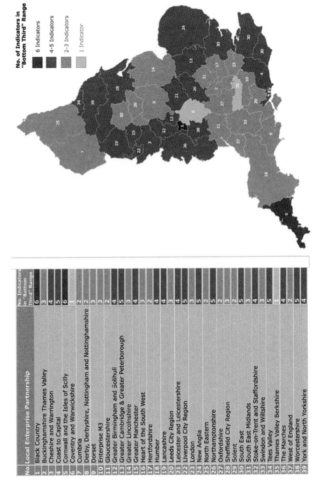

No. of Indicators in "Bottom Third" Range
- 6 Indicators
- 4-5 Indicators
- 2-3 Indicators
- 1 Indicator

No	Local Enterprise Partnership	No. of Indicators in "Bottom Third" Range
1	Black Country	6
2	Buckinghamshire Thames Valley	3
3	Cheshire and Warrington	4
4	Coast to Capital	5
5	Cornwall and the Isles of Scilly	6
6	Coventry and Warwickshire	1
7	Cumbria	2
8	Derby, Derbyshire, Nottingham and Nottinghamshire	2
9	Dorset	3
10	Enterprise M3	3
11	Gloucestershire	2
12	Greater Birmingham and Solihull	4
13	Greater Cambridge & Greater Peterborough	5
14	Greater Lincolnshire	3
15	Greater Manchester	4
16	Heart of the South West	3
17	Hertfordshire	2
18	Humber	4
19	Lancashire	4
20	Leeds City Region	3
21	Leicester and Leicestershire	4
22	Liverpool City Region	5
23	London	3
24	New Anglia	5
25	North Eastern	2
26	Northamptonshire	5
27	Oxfordshire	3
28	Sheffield City Region	2
29	Solent	2
30	South East	5
31	South East Midlands	3
32	Stoke-on-Trent and Staffordshire	4
33	Swindon and Wiltshire	3
34	Tees Valley	5
35	Thames Valley Berkshire	1
36	The Marches	4
37	West of England	2
38	Worcestershire	5
39	York and North Yorkshire	4

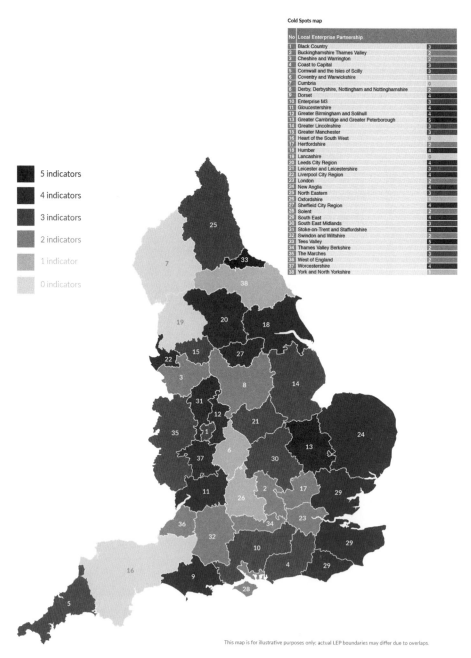

Cold Spots map

No	Local Enterprise Partnership	
1	Black Country	3
2	Buckinghamshire Thames Valley	2
3	Cheshire and Warrington	2
4	Coast to Capital	3
5	Cornwall and the Isles of Scilly	3
6	Coventry and Warwickshire	1
7	Cumbria	0
8	Derby, Derbyshire, Nottingham and Nottinghamshire	2
9	Dorset	4
10	Enterprise M3	3
11	Gloucestershire	4
12	Greater Birmingham and Solihull	4
13	Greater Cambridge and Greater Peterborough	5
14	Greater Lincolnshire	3
15	Greater Manchester	3
16	Heart of the South West	0
17	Hertfordshire	2
18	Humber	4
19	Lancashire	0
20	Leeds City Region	4
21	Leicester and Leicestershire	3
22	Liverpool City Region	4
23	London	2
24	New Anglia	4
25	North Eastern	3
26	Oxfordshire	1
27	Sheffield City Region	4
28	Solent	2
29	South East	4
30	South East Midlands	3
31	Stoke-on-Trent and Staffordshire	4
32	Swindon and Wiltshire	2
33	Tees Valley	5
34	Thames Valley Berkshire	2
35	The Marches	3
36	West of England	2
37	Worcestershire	4
38	York and North Yorkshire	1

- ■ 5 indicators
- ■ 4 indicators
- ■ 3 indicators
- ■ 2 indicators
- ■ 1 indicator
- ■ 0 indicators

This map is for illustrative purposes only; actual LEP boundaries may differ due to overlaps.

Some of the shift relative to last year is not a change in performance but driven by losing two of the indicators. The model is therefore weighted stronger towards education than the labour market and areas with a stronger performance in these indicators will appear lighter. That is why we are also looking at change since 2015.

Source: Careers and Enterprise Company (2018). *Updating the Careers Cold Spots: The Careers and Enterprise Prioritisation Indicators*, p. 4. Available at: https://www.careersandenterprise.co.uk/sites/default/files/uploaded/updating_the_careers_cold_spots_report.pdf.

being taught about colonialism in his family's native India as his *first* introduction to history:

Just as the India I was taught about was different to the India I am descended from, the university on my doorstep was very different to the Manchester I grew up in. [...] Quite often in big cities like Manchester, huge universities are close to areas with low progression into university, and the communities nearby benefit least from these gigantic institutions.[16]

Nagdee chanced upon an information session about an access programme when he accompanied a friend 'lured by the promise of food'![17] Twice a month Nagdee attended workshops at the university:

One in particular stands out to me. I had to work in a group with other seventeen- and eighteen-year-olds and prepare a presentation. It was only when I was on stage that it dawned on me that I had never done any form of public speaking before, and I panicked.[18]

After gaining the grades to study at the University of Manchester, Nagdee says:

I knew one of the first things I wanted to do was work with young people from backgrounds like mine: young, working-class kids who thought they had no chance in hell of going to university.[19]

Nagdee was the National Union of Students (NUS) Black Students' Officer between 2017 and 2019, representing, campaigning on behalf of, and advocating for BAME students. Nagdee also mentions the Birmingham Black Ambassadors Scheme (which has evolved into the Birmingham BME Student Ambassador Programme)[20], which recruits

---

16 Ilyas Nagdee, 'Half-Truth Histories: How Erasing Empire Maintains the Status Quo'. In Nikesh Shukla and Sammy Jones (eds), *RIFE: Twenty-One Stories from Britain's Youth* (London: Unbound, 2019), pp. 193–209 at p. 200.
17 Nagdee, 'Half-Truth Histories', p. 199.
18 Nagdee, 'Half-Truth Histories', p. 199. Communication skills are one of the seven skills highlighted by Tony Wagner in *The Global Achievement Gap*.
19 Nagdee, 'Half-Truth Histories', p. 200.
20 Nagdee, 'Half-Truth Histories', p. 208.

BAME students to support their peers and work in schools to high-light the university route.

What if you're at an independent school and you're expected to do A levels and go on to university? What if you don't feel suited to the academic route and feel that something more practical and hands-on would suit you better? Studying at Millfield School in Somerset, Charlotte Wilson is undertaking a BTEC in enterprise and entrepreneurship and an A level in media. She intended to study three A levels after GCSEs, but says:

The minute I heard about the BTec I was instantly excited. It is really hands-on, the challenges really excited me. It was a risk as I hadn't done GCSE business [...] I have three teachers and get on really well with all of them. They helped me really develop, how to present and communicate properly.[21]

Charlotte's experience is another example of stereotypes being tackled – this time by choosing a less academic/more vocational route for post-16 education, thanks to the teachers at her school.

The Times reports complaints from an independent school head, Andrew Hall from King's College School in Wimbledon, that Oxford and Cambridge universities 'operate "an unofficial quota system" for pupils from state schools, even if they have inferior A-level results'.[22] Hall is claiming – without irony – that (after years of his students presumably getting in on 'merit') there is an 'unofficial cap of 30% on private-school pupils' at both universities, which was introduced in summer 2019. (It is worth noting that although privately educated students in the UK account for just 7% of the total school population, their proportion of places taken at Oxbridge in recent years has been 'just under 40%'. Presumably Mr Hall doesn't think this is unfair?)

In the 21st century, there is systemic inequality in education in the UK, in that parents who can afford to move into the catchment area of grammar schools or outstanding state schools afford their children an advantage over children in state schools and academies in other areas.

---

21 Rosemary Bennett, Case Study: 'The Minute I Heard About the BTec I Was Instantly Excited', *The Times* (24 August). Available at: https://thetimes.co.uk/article/case-study-the-minute-i-heard-about-the-btec-i-was-instantly-excited-plk8nqgzn.
22 Sian Griffiths, Oxbridge 'Penalises' Private School Pupils, *The Times* (25 August 2019). Available at: https://thetimes.co.uk/article/oxbridge-penalises-private-school-pupils-m89dpbmqp.

Looking at the headlines from the August 2019 GCSE results, there is some good news in that female entries to GCSE computing rose by 14% to 21.4% of overall entries at 17,158; however, this is still way below the 62,869 male entries. Performance-wise, 24.9% of girls received the top grade, compared to the 20.8% of boys scoring top grades. The proportion of GCSEs awarded top grades rose for the second year, and 20.8% of GCSE entries scored one of the top three grades, as opposed to 20.5% in 2018.[23]

Unfortunately, research shows that disadvantaged pupils are almost twice as likely to fail GCSE maths as their wealthier classmates. Analysis carried out by education charity Teach First found that students from poorer backgrounds in England and Wales are 'lagging far behind their wealthier peers in key subjects at GCSE'.[24] Russell Hobby, chief executive of Teach First, said:

A child's postcode should never determine how well they do at school, yet today we've seen huge disparities based on just that. Low attainment at GCSE is a real cause for concern as it can shut doors to future success and hold young people back from meeting their aspirations.[25]

Quite. The 2019 GCSE analysis showed that 38% of pupils from the poorest one-third of postcodes in England and Wales fail GCSE maths whereas nearly half as many (20%) fail GCSE maths from the wealthiest third of postcodes.[26] Educational inequality is not new. Theresa May, in her 'great meritocracy' speech on 9 September 2016, suggests inequality is maintained through selective schools being in areas which deny those who can't afford to move house. She says 'so we help no one – not least those who can't afford to move house or pay for a private education – by saying to parents who want a selective education for their child that we won't let them have it.'[27] These comments also mirror the findings of the cold-spots research, which

23 Frances Perraudin, GCSE Results Day 2019: Increase in Top Grades – Live, *The Guardian* (22 August 2019). Available at: https://www.theguardian.com/education/live/2019/aug/22/gcse-results-day-2019-live-news.
24 Reported in Sally Weale, Poorer Pupils Twice as Likely to Fail Key GCSEs, *The Guardian* (21 August 2019). Available at: https://www.theguardian.com/education/2019/aug/21/poorer-pupils-twice-as-likely-to-fail-key-gcses.
25 Quoted in Weale, Poorer Pupils Twice as Likely to Fail Key GCSEs.
26 Quoted in Weale, Poorer Pupils Twice as Likely to Fail Key GCSEs.
27 Theresa May, 'The Great Meritocracy: Prime Minister's Speech', 9 September 2016. Available at: https://www.gov.uk/government/speeches/britain-the-great-meritocracy-prime-ministers-speech.

suggests that poor academic attainment goes hand-in-hand with higher proportions of free school meals and lower levels of business engagement in schools.[28]

Apprenticeships and skills

What if you attend school which is seen as 'academic' so doesn't offer apprenticeship information as part of careers learning? What if your school deems certain students 'non-academic', and so the only suggestion offered is to go to college to study a 'vocational skill'? 'Vocational' does, of course, mean 'practical and creative' but, alarmingly, it can be used as a synonym for 'badly behaved' or 'non-academic'.

Apprenticeships have had a reasonably positive, and loudly trumpeted, renaissance in the past decade – with modest increases in people undertaking apprenticeships in manufacturing and engineering (from 70,000 in 2011/12 to around 73,000 in 2016/17);[29] of this number, the majority of apprenticeships (in engineering, for example) have been at Levels 2 or 3, despite the majority of all apprentices being 19 and over, which possibly suggests that the current workforce is being upskilled, rather than bringing in new learners as entrants to the apprenticeship model.[30]

The Royal Academy of Engineering outlines how higher level apprenticeships are equivalent to engineering degrees, so this is certainly not a second-rate course of study and one which should be brought to students' attention by their careers advisors and teachers, or by external sources such as companies or third sector organisations.[31] One of the key recommendations from the 2013 Perkins Review was:

The engineering community should provide continuing professional development for teachers, giving them experience of working in industry to develop the knowledge to put their academic teaching in practical context [...] as well as enabling them to inspire and inform their students about engineering.[32]

28 Careers and Enterprise Company, *Prioritisation Index 2015*.
29 Royal Academy of Engineering, *Engineering Skills for the Future*, p. 38.
30 Royal Academy of Engineering, *Engineering Skills for the Future*, p. 8.
31 Royal Academy of Engineering, *Engineering Skills for the Future*, p. 34.
32 Royal Academy of Engineering, *Engineering Skills for the Future*, p. 14.

Since this was issued as a recommendation in 2013, 231 industry and HE placements have been delivered for teachers and 24 lead schools have been supported by the Institute of Physics to drive improvements in physics teaching. This is not enough, and to be fair the Royal Academy of Engineering rates this as 'Amber: some progress made since 2013.'[33] Well, there are 6,811 secondary schools in England (3,448 mainstream, 1,044 special and 2,391 independent),[34] so supporting 231 teachers and 24 schools in one subject area isn't even picking up the pin to scratch the surface.

Further research by the Institute of Physics looked into gender imbalances in STEM subjects.[35] The research, using data from the national pupil database, looked at the gender balance across a number of A level subjects in co-educational schools. Some of the main findings include:

- Nearly half of co-educational state-funded schools (49%) are actually making the gender imbalance in these subjects worse.

- The small number of schools (19%) that send on relatively more girls to do A level physics also have a smaller gender imbalance in progression to other subjects.

- If girls are dissuaded from studying A level physics, it may be exacerbated by the subject or school approach in that setting.

This research highlights that not only is there a gender gap in many STEM subjects, but that in some schools it's actually getting worse.

Schools in the UK do not compel students to continue with separate science subjects at GCSE. Subject choices made at 16 in England, Wales and Northern Ireland often effectively are between sciences/maths and arts/humanities, tending to lead to some students being effectively 'cut off' from STEM subjects at A level, possibly before they understand how these subjects could support many different career routes later in life.[36] The Royal Academy of Engineering suggests that a broader curriculum (like the English or Welsh Baccalaureate) 'develops students' understanding of 21st century challenges and

---

33 Royal Academy of Engineering, *Engineering Skills for the Future*, p. 13.
34 Department for Education, Schools, Pupils and Their Characteristics [statistical release] (January 2019), p. 5. Available at: https://assets.publishing.service.gov.uk/government/uploads/system/uploads/attachment_data/file/812539/Schools_Pupils_and_their_Characteristics_2019_Main_Text.pdf.
35 Frances Saunders, *Closing Doors: Exploring Gender and Subject Choice in Schools*, An Institute of Physics report (December 2013). Available at: http://www.iop.org/education/teacher/support/girls_physics/closing-doors/page_62076.html.
36 Royal Academy of Engineering, *Engineering Skills for the Future*, pp. 6–7.

enhances *engineering habits of mind* skills such as problem solving, creativity and critical thinking'.[37] (All of which are also components of Tony Wagner's research.[38])

A broad and balanced curriculum is also advocated for by the Royal Society who, in February 2019, called for an independent review of post-16 education because 'A-levels are not giving today's young people the best start for getting good jobs in the future.'[39] The Royal Society found that 80% of businesses expect to increase the number of high-skilled roles over the coming years but around 65% are concerned there will be a lack of sufficiently skilled young people to fill them.

In an address to business leaders, Royal Society president Venki Ramakrishnan presented research which finds that:

You are more than twice as likely to be studying four or more A-levels if you are a student not eligible for free school meals. You are more than three time as likely to be studying 4 or more A-levels if you are at a private or Grammar school rather than a Comprehensive and you are more than twice as likely if you live in the South East as opposed to the North East. Sadly, this is all too predictable. [...] Careers are becoming more flexible and we need to change expectations of what a person's 'career', or more likely 'careers', will look like. Businesses need employees with a broad range of skills and experience that can help them to creatively adapt to a rapidly changing and technology-rich world.[40]

Speaking at the same event, Carolyn Fairbairn, director general of the Confederation of British Industry (CBI), said:

The need to best prepare our young people for work has never been more important. The growing need for higher level skill is already holding some firms back.[41]

---

37 Royal Academy of Engineering, *Engineering Skills for the Future*, p. 27.
38 Wagner, *The Global Achievement Gap*.
39 Royal Society, Royal Society Calls for Independent Review of Post-16 Education (12 February 2019). Available at: https://royalsociety.org/news/2019/02/call-for-independent-review-of-post-16-education/.
40 Royal Society, Royal Society Calls for Independent Review of Post-16 Education.
41 Royal Society, Royal Society Calls for Independent Review of Post-16 Education.

The annual report of Her Majesty's Chief Inspector also notes a mismatch between the government's Industrial Strategy – with the focus on AI, ageing society, clean growth and the future of mobility – and the corresponding skills-led apprenticeships.[42] Amanda Spielman states:

Business management and health accounted for almost half of all higher-level apprenticeships started in 2018/19. This does not appear to align well with our grand challenges as a country.[43]

OK, so it's not *just* STEM subjects that are important and it's not *just* skills for work that are important, but here are two major internationally respected organisations – the CBI and the Royal Society – agreeing that we need to increase breadth and options, not stream students too early and focus on their developing *skills* for the future. Changing the curriculum won't happen overnight, but increased awareness of apprenticeships and baccalaureates will help students and shine headlights down different roads ahead. However, much of the required change comes down to broader, more contextualised learning in *all* subject areas and a focus on the *skills* that young people are developing. (And not just the skills, but also how the young person *habitually* recognises, recalls and 'owns' their skills.)

In November 2016 Angela Rayner, Labour's then shadow secretary of state for education, noted that almost a quarter of a million students entered university in 2015, yet 'if you were to listen to the policy debate about education, you could be forgiven for believing every 18-year-old was going to university'.[44] Typically, headline figures about post-18 destinations focus on university; however, says Rayner, we 'must start by understanding that if 31 per cent of young people are going to university, then 69 per cent are not.'[45] Rayner also notes how, in her 2016 Labour Party Conference speech, she 'called out the snobbery towards vocational education that exists too often amongst

---

42 See https://www.gov.uk/government/topical-events/the-uks-industrial-strategy.
43 Ofsted, *The Annual Report of Her Majesty's Chief Inspector of Education, Children's Services and Skills 2018/19*. Ref: HC 28 2018-19 (2020), p. 26. Available at: https://assets. publishing.service.gov.uk/government/uploads/system/uploads/attachment_data/ file/859422/Annual_Report_of_Her_Majesty_s_Chief_Inspector_of_Education__ Children_s_Services_and_Skills_201819.pdf.
44 Angela Rayner, We Must Be Serious About Vocational Education, *New Statesman – Spotlight, Skills: Training for the New Economy* (11 November 2016), p. 6. Available at: https://www.newstatesman.com/sites/default/files/skills_supplement_11th_ nov_2016_0.pdf.
45 Rayner, We Must Be Serious About Vocational Education, p. 6.

the great and the good'.[46] Another issue is that some schools are resistant to highlight pathways that could take students away from their own sixth forms and towards local FE colleges and employers.

Finally, apprenticeships are another aspect of FE and HE, and another pathway to a fulfilling career. They are often sold as 'debt-free' or 'earn whilst you learn' – surely the best of both worlds? Maybe, maybe not; it depends on the perception of apprenticeships and their benefits and usefulness.

Parents were found to have somewhat negative views of the role and benefits of apprenticeships, as ABM UK found in their research in 2018.[47] Interviewing 2,000 parents and 2,000 11–15-year-olds, they found that 43% of parents felt apprenticeships were poorly paid and saw them as a second-rate option for young people who failed their exams.

Research by the trade union Unison 'suggests health service employers are plugging staffing gaps with apprentices in return for low pay and minimal on-the-job training'.[48] On average, the apprentices surveyed were earning less than £4 an hour, despite performing a similar range of tasks to salaried employees. Earning whilst you learn may be a good idea in theory but some employers will find ways to save money where possible, and apprenticeships could be seen as a subsidised scheme which benefits employers by paying less than the minimum wage.

A survey commissioned by the Chartered Management Institute (CMI) in 2019 found that 51% would encourage their child to apply for an apprenticeship instead of university and 59% of parents thought an apprenticeship provided better job prospects than a university degree.[49]

Rob Wall, head of policy at the CMI, said that 'despite the positive results, our survey shows that more still needs to be done to change perceptions and raise awareness of apprenticeships'.

---

46 Rayner, We Must Be Serious About Vocational Education, p. 6.
47 Chris Townsend, Do You Mind the Gap? *This Week in FM* (5 March 2019). Available at: https://www.twinfm.com/article/do-you-mind-the-gap.
48 Unison, NHS Exploiting Apprentices through Low Pay, Warns UNISON [press release] (24 April 2016). Available at: https://www.unison.org.uk/news/press-release/2016/04/nhs-exploiting-apprentices-through-low-pay-warns-unison/.
49 Chartered Management Institute, Apprenticeships Make the Grade [press release] (14 August 2019). Available at: https://www.managers.org.uk/about-us/media-centre/cmi-press-releases/apprenticeships-make-the-grade.

Wall also hinted at frustration, saying: 'we need a better careers system to signpost the full range of options available and to end the snobbery that still exists in parts of the education system that apprenticeships are somehow a second-class option'.[50]

CEIAG opens eyes and minds

The other side of this coin is the damaging myth that 'university/ apprenticeships/[insert whatever preconceived notion seldom based on fact here] isn't for the likes of us'. These views have persisted for years and were studied by the Sutton Trust and the Department for Business, Innovation and Skills in 2009. They found that pupils from top independent schools make twice as many applications to leading research universities as their comprehensive school peers with comparable grades. Sir Peter Lampl, founder and chairman of Sutton Trust, said, 'Many highly able pupils from non-privileged backgrounds wrongly perceive universities are "not for the likes of us" and often lack the support and guidance to overcome this suggestion.'[51] The research found that 'low application rates are a considerable factor in the relatively low entry into selective research universities from state maintained schools and from FE colleges' but the research could not conclusively suggest why this was occurring. It posits that it could be that 'students attending institutions with relatively little experience of successful applications to selective universities may be less well able to support their students in terms of factors such as subject choices, preparing applications and personal statements'.[52]

See? There it is again – a lack of support and guidance, a lack of self-belief and, underpinning that, family backgrounds where no one has even applied, let alone gone, to university. Inequality exists in many forms.

Independent (or private/public) schools – the fee-paying ones – are also able to create more advantages for their students through their various networks. Connections create conversations which lead to

---

50 Chartered Management Institute, Apprenticeships Make the Grade.
51 Quoted in Rebecca Attwood, 'Not for the Likes of Us', *Times Higher Education* (12 August 2009). Available at: https://timeshighereducation.com/news/not-for-the-likes-of-us/407750.article.
52 Sutton Trust and the Department for Business, Innovation and Skills, *Applications, Offers and Admissions to Research-Led Universities*, BIS Research Paper No. 5 (August 2009), p. 21. Available at: https://www.suttontrust.com/wp-content/uploads/2019/12/BIS_ST_report-1.pdf.

inspiration. What do I mean by that? Research carried out by Speakers4Schools and the Education and Employers charity found that independent schools leverage strong social capital which enables them to invite leaders from across public life to speak to students, alongside their alumni connections and parental networks.[53] Robert Peston says:

When I created Speakers4Schools in 2010, it was because I was infuriated that only the leading independent schools were asking me to give talks to their students, rather than the kind of state school that gave me a great and grounded education in the 1970s. [...] Schools that engage with speakers from programmes like ours are more likely to foster confidence and ambition in their students.[54]

The research found that the vast majority of young people were positive about the benefits of talks in areas such as motivation, attitudes, understanding career paths and self-belief – 88% responded that the talks had helped them to see how to overcome setbacks.[55] The talks also had a higher impact on students supported by free school meals (with self-efficacy being positively impacted). As we have seen, it is especially important that students can see that 'people like me' can succeed in professions previously thought of as out of reach.

Teachers also reported positive benefits of schools inviting speakers in, including feeling 'far more likely' to believe that their school was doing enough to prepare their young people for the future. Teachers in schools that offered talks had 171% higher odds of being confident in their school's career provision than those in schools that didn't.[56] Schools exhibiting the most benefits allowed students to interact with speakers in Q&A sessions, prepared students with details about the speaker's background beforehand, invited speakers based on who the *students* wanted to hear from, and allowed time to discuss the session afterwards.

---

53 Christian Percy, Jordan Rehill, Elnaz Kashefpakdel, Nick Chambers, Ashley Hodges and Max Haskins, *Insight and Inspiration: Evaluating the Impact on Guest Speakers in Schools* (London: Education and Employers and Speakers4Schools, 2019). Available at: https://www.educationandemployers.org/wp-content/uploads/2019/10/Insights-and-Inspiration-Exploring-the-impact-of-guest-speakers-in-schools-1.pdf.
54 Percy et al., *Insight and Inspiration*, p. 2.
55 Percy et al., *Insight and Inspiration*, p. 4.
56 Percy et al., *Insight and Inspiration*, p. 5.

It is estimated that there are likely to be around 70,000 internships offered by UK companies annually.[57] Research shows that over 40% of young people who have carried out an internship have done so unpaid. The Higher Education Statistics Agency (HESA) showed that, in 2017, of roughly 10,000 graduates who were undertaking an internship six months post-graduation, 20% of them were doing so unpaid. Official internships qualify for at least the minimum wage in the UK, but there are a number of caveats which can be used to reduce or deny payment.[58] The Sutton Trust's own analysis found that the minimum cost to an intern is £1,019 per month in London and £827 in Manchester.[59]

In the developed world, and in a democracy, aren't we supposed to have choice over what we do, what we achieve and what we aspire to become? A democracy is supposedly a meritocracy, yet so often our life chances and choices are restricted, determined or amplified by geography, birth and/or education. Isn't it right then, that we – as educators, mentors, guides and parents – do as much as we can to level the playing field and provide appropriate, aspirational vision and opportunity for all students?

Young adults would have welcomed greater preparation for the working world from their schools and colleges, with the greatest demand coming from young women and adults from disadvantaged backgrounds. The greatest skills demand was for practical information and job-finding skills. These were the findings of research into transitions commissioned by Education and Employers.[60] We need to make sure that we inform *all* students of *all* ages – regardless of ability or background – of *all* of the pathways, opportunities and futures that are open to them as they progress through education and into employment, entrepreneurship or self-employment.

---

57 Rebecca Montacute, Internships: Unpaid, Unadvertised, Unfair. Sutton Trust research brief, edition 20 (January 2018), p. 1. Available at: https://www.suttontrust.com/wp-content/uploads/2018/01/Internships-2018-briefing-1.pdf.
58 See https://www.gov.uk/employment-rights-for-interns.
59 Montacute, *Internships: Unpaid, Unadvertised, Unfair*, p. 1.
60 Anthony Mann, Elnaz T. Kashefpakdel, Jordan Rehill and Prue Huddleston, *Contemporary Transitions: Young Britons Reflect on Life After Secondary School and College*, Education and Employers Occasional Research Paper 11 (September 2017). Available at: https://www.educationandemployers.org/wp-content/uploads/2017/01/Contemporary-Transitions-30-01-2017.pdf.

Conclusion

Careers education is not a one-size-fits-all approach. Careers education isn't a single solution and, as we have seen from the research cited in this chapter, we need to make sure that as much good-quality careers advice and guidance is delivered, as often as possible, in as many varied ways as possible, and linked to as many subjects and industries as possible. More than that, we need to advocate for, coach and support young people to equip them to rise to the challenges that they might not *yet* be ready to face by helping them to create powerful resources and habits of mind. We need to help them to prepare to undertake the steps necessary to succeed in their *chosen* career, whatever that career and those steps might be.

What could you do *today* to help a young person overcome a difficulty or an inequality?

Because if not you, then who?

Chapter 4

APPLYING THE GATSBY BENCHMARKS

The best schools have a sign above the door regardless of what context they are working in, which says, 'This is how we do it here' […] The best schools have absolute consistency.

Paul Dix[1]

Dix is talking about behaviour, but this approach to culture is essential across all elements of a school. In any setting, leadership is key. Without true leadership and a set of guiding principles for staff to follow, culture is left to chance and a culture left to chance makes its own rules.

School culture is essential when talking about careers education because it is typically only delivered at particular stages (before work experience, just before leaving school or as students apply to university). It has not always been a statutory requirement and frequently not part of any official assessments. Statutory guidance does, however, make it clear that 'a successful careers guidance programme will also be reflected in higher numbers of pupils progressing to positive destinations'.[2] In this regard, the school's culture in relation to careers education is vitally important to better student futures.

---

1   Paul Dix, *When the Adults Change, Everything Changes: Seismic Shifts in School Behaviour* (Carmarthen: Independent Thinking Press, 2017), p. 4.
2   Department for Education, *Careers Guidance and Access for Education and Training Providers*, p. 6.

The benchmarks

Since the Gatsby Benchmarks were created in 2014, they have become an established tool to develop, assess, apply and measure careers education in schools, hence why I recommend that schools adopt them alongside the CASK. The eight-part model of what schools need to cover as part of excellent careers education is as follows:

1. A stable careers programme.

2. Learning from career and labour market information.

3. Addressing the needs of each pupil.

4. Linking curriculum learning to careers.

5. Encounters with employers and employees.

6. Experiences of workplaces.

7. Encounters with further and higher education.

8. Personal guidance.[3]

The foundation also highlights the push and pull factors inherent in good careers guidance:

*   Push: based in school/education setting and 'include good information and careers education, personal guidance tailored to individual needs and, above all, inspiring teaching that gives pupils the right qualifications'.[4] Doesn't just point students towards university but allows them a broad range of career options and pathways to consider.

*   Pull: 'factors come from employers who show pupils what the workplace is like and inspire them with the opportunities of work, through measures including direct work experience, meeting employers and employees in person.'[5]

There is a lot to consider, so let's pick out a few examples from the Gatsby guidance document and highlight some ways in which to achieve the benchmarks.

---

3   Gatsby Charitable Foundation, *Good Career Guidance*, p. 7.
4   Gatsby Charitable Foundation, *Good Career Guidance*, p. 19.
5   Gatsby Charitable Foundation, *Good Career Guidance*, p. 31.

Benchmark 1: a stable careers programme

The first of the Gatsby Benchmarks, and key amongst them, is defined as 'an embedded programme of career education and guidance that is known and understood by pupils, parents, teachers, governors and employers.'[6] In short, a culture of careers education which *has* to come from the SLT in any setting.

Once an SLT lead for careers and enterprise is in place – and the role is seen as a critical part of the learning and reporting structures of the school – then adoption of the programme into the curriculum can take place through the careers lead, subject leaders and a lead governor for careers. Once part of the appraisal and reporting system throughout the establishment, simple methods for inclusion and review can be conducted as part of planning and reflection by the students and staff teams.

Benchmark 2: learning from career and labour market information

Just as parents are often seen as 'out of touch' by their teenage children with regard to fashion, music and hairstyles, they are equally likely to be out of touch for providing careers advice based on up-to-date information and trends in the labour market. This is likely to also be true of busy subject teachers in secondary schools (unless they have discovered the ability to make time).

Thankfully, the internet provides many sources of information on careers trends, skills needs and the future of any number of jobs. There are myriad sources of data and employment trends in multiple industries in countries across the world. Sometimes it's narrowing down the avalanche of stats that can be the difficult thing to do.

Enabling students to access sources of information such as the National Careers Service[7] will enable them to find out the details, requirements and future opportunities in a vast range of careers. The information provided can be searched by skills, qualification pathways and local needs.

---

6   Gatsby Charitable Foundation, *Good Career Guidance*, p. 7.
7   See https://nationalcareers.service.gov.uk.

In the quickly changing world of work, it is more useful than ever to refer to reliable sources of information to help young people plan their futures.

Other sources of labour market information are:

- LMI For All – a Government website which collates useful objective sources of labour market information (LMI): https://www.lmiforall.org.uk/explore_lmi/learning-units/sources_of_lmi/
- National Careers Week: www.nationalcareersweek.com
- BBC Bitesize Careers: https://www.bbc.co.uk/bitesize/careers

Benchmark 3: addressing the needs of each pupil

'A school's careers programme should actively seek to challenge stereotypical thinking and raise aspirations.'[8] This is desirable, of course, but it's hard to do if you're not *the* careers teacher or advisor. However, you can make sure that you challenge the usual perceptions at play in careers sessions, in which stereotypes can sometimes slip through – for example, in the gendered language that we use. When talking about firefighters, for example, we might, more often than not, say fireman, rather than firefighter, or when speaking about company directors we will often say 'he' rather than 'he or she'.

That is not the only way in which we can broaden students' views of careers. The Gatsby report found that in some independent schools in particular, students struggled to name a STEM professional that wasn't a doctor! In some instances, teachers had to temper students' questions and their advice with realism and try to support students to *reduce* their aspirations.

Benchmark 4: linking curriculum learning to careers

In the Netherlands, *Technasium* networks allow students to elect to spend 20% of their time on problem-based learning. They work in teams to solve real-life problems set by local businesses. This is similar to the recent development of UTCs in the UK, which are

---

8   Gatsby Charitable Foundation, *Good Career Guidance*, p. 22.

generally sponsored by a large local employer or industry in order to facilitate the training and development of young people undertaking BTEC or apprenticeship qualifications. This obviously supports the needs of Benchmark 4; however, UTCs do seem to have suffered from significant sponsorship and retention issues in the years running up to 2020.

It is reported that 91% of apprentices are retained by the company that trains them, which suggests that those who undertake an apprenticeship are likely to progress into full-time work.[9] For me, this highlights the importance of apprising young people of careers through the curriculum to ensure a higher likelihood of long-term career happiness.

Teachers in Ontario and Finland, for example, are expected to relate careers to their subjects whilst teaching: 'Teachers of science and mathematics can increase the relevance of their teaching and foster career learning'.[10] However, sometimes the aspiration runs ahead of the practice. As in the UK, patchy practice highlights how delivery of this benchmark is heavily dependent on the classroom teacher's experience of past careers and their understanding of the job market:

Yet the opportunities are clearly there: subject teachers see far more of their pupils than guidance specialists do and often have a close relationship with them. Subject teachers can often be powerful role models to attract pupils towards their subject and the careers that flow from it.[11]

Yes, teachers *can* be powerful role models, but teachers are busy, the school year is cyclical and full of pressure points, and often the curriculum takes up all of the available time. Arguably the subject teacher's focus should be on their subject, but a working knowledge of careers which use that subject is also valuable. Indeed, it's necessary to support students' broader longer-term learning and understanding.

---

9   Magda Knight, Are Apprenticeships Worth It? 6 Questions You're Secretly Asking (And Their Myth-Busting Answers), *Youth Employment UK* (6 March 2018). Available at: https://www.youthemployment.org.uk/are-apprenticeships-worth-it-myths-facts/.
10 Gatsby Charitable Foundation, *Good Career Guidance*, p. 23.
11 Gatsby Charitable Foundation, *Good Career Guidance*, p. 23.

Benchmark 5: encounters with employers and employees

Benchmark 5 is, according to the research, an important one. Whether this is in the form of assemblies, careers fairs, activities put on by local businesses within the school or enterprise activities with industrial themes, these encounters help students to explore what 'work' is actually like. Encounters with employers and employees keep students up to date on the real world of work, and offer more current and realistic viewpoints than the snapshots they've picked up from peers, teachers, parents and other sources, such as media, films and TV. Crucially, research carried out by Anthony Mann found that:

The 7% of young adults surveyed who recalled four or more [career-based] activities while at school were five times less likely to be NEET and earned, on average, 16% more than peers who recalled no such activities.[12]

The statutory guidance is also clear on the benefits of Benchmark 5: 'Schools should engage fully with local employers, businesses and professional networks to ensure real-world connections with employers lie at the heart of the careers strategy.' In the same paragraph they speak about the importance of visiting speakers who can more readily relate to young people: 'Visiting speakers can include quite junior employees, or apprentices, particularly alumni, with whom pupils can readily identify'.[13]

Visits from alumni are also key to delivering Benchmark 5. Well-developed in the USA and in independent schools across the UK, this is a valuable resource that's largely untapped in non-selective state schools. (As an aside, going back to my school was the last thing that I – and the school, probably – wanted. However, now I am of a more mature disposition, and age, I've returned to talk to the sixth form about how *not* to approach your studies. Seeing as I've been asked back four or five times, there seems to be mutual benefit.)

Future First is a charity set up to support and facilitate state schools in establishing their own alumni networks.[14] It is a fantastic concept,

---

12 Mann, It's Who You Meet, p. 1.
13 Department for Education, *Careers Guidance and Access for Education and Training Providers*, p. 26.
14 See https://futurefirst.org.uk.

which helps to build aspiration and provide visible – and, crucially, relatable – role models. In research published in 2019, Future First found that 65% of young people worry about what job they will do as adults and '71% of young people said it would be helpful if they could meet students that went to their school and talk to them about what they did after education and in their jobs.'[15]

Tristram Hooley says:

Better career education and guidance and a strengthening of the culture of placements, as well as employer engagement in the education system, will undoubtedly help to improve the relationship between education and employment.[16]

This represents a definite advocacy of Benchmark 5, and we can see the importance of relationships, employer involvement and skills development alongside academic achievements.

Benchmark 6: experiences of workplaces

Relating to Benchmark 6, Gatsby are very clear that in the countries they visited to gather evidence for the report, 'There is good evidence of the impact of work experience in giving pupils a more realistic idea of the workplace'.[17] One of the recommendations is that schools have at least one employer governor to oversee engagement, because, 'Governors are well placed to act as brokers between schools and employers.'[18] Governors are willing volunteers, will often be retired and will have decades of contacts and experiences to draw upon – so make this work for your students in relation to careers advice and support.

---

15 Future First, *Young People, Their Futures and Access to Relatable Role Models* (September 2019). p. 2. Available at: https://futurefirst.org.uk/blog/young-people-their-futures-and-access-to-relatable-role-models/.

16 Tristram Hooley, Can HE Single-Handedly Solve Skills Shortages? *WonkHE* [blog] (9 September 2019). Available at: https://wonkhe.com/blogs/can-higher-education-single-handedly-solve-skills-shortages/.

17 Gatsby Charitable Foundation, *Good Career Guidance*, p. 26.

18 Gatsby Charitable Foundation, *Good Career Guidance*, p. 53.

Benchmark 7: encounters with further and higher education

Gatsby recommend increasing the number and frequency of encounters between young people and their slightly older peers from FE and HE. Universities are required to engage in school outreach through their access agreements with the Office for Fair Access (OFFA). Schools need to make the most of this and should contact local universities to ask for support, which will be offered in a variety of ways – from events within the school to open days, careers fairs and school visits from student ambassadors.

There is often central government funding available to support interactions with schools, especially for students who would consider university as being out of reach. Uni Connect (formerly the National Collaborative Outreach Programme (NCOP)) is administered by local partnerships to reach students in specific wards and postcodes defined as suffering from multiple deprivations.[19] Although national, the application of the scheme seems somewhat patchy. Local colleges and apprenticeship providers should also get involved in sending ambassadors into schools. This is even more powerful if the ambassador is an alumnus of the school, as Gatsby state that:

When a young person meets another who has come from the same background and has gone onto success, that can motivate them in a way that encounters with older people cannot.[20]

Benchmark 8: personal guidance

Alongside the input that all schools will endeavour to offer to their young people, how do you know whether the activities and initiatives are having an impact on each student? How will you know whether that inspirational assembly or work experience has led to them making any concrete decisions? How will you know if your efforts have been in vain and Connor in Year 10 still hasn't got a clue where his future might lie?

---

19 See https://www.officeforstudents.org.uk/advice-and-guidance/promoting-equal-opportunities/uni-connect/.
20 Gatsby Charitable Foundation, *Good Career Guidance*, p. 54.

Well, this is the role of personal guidance – which should happen at least once – to discuss each individual student's aspirations and careers awareness with them and to support them in taking their next steps. (This may, of course, also mean discussing more realistic options *or* having an honest exchange about their performance and the likelihood of the success of their future plans).

The Gatsby Foundation recommends that 'the interview should be with an adviser who is appropriately trained to have the necessary guidance skills, the knowledge of information sources and the essential impartiality to do the job'.[21] Neither the statutory guidance nor the benchmarks set out any compulsory regulations about who should conduct the guidance interview, but there is an expectation that the advisor will be a professional and well-versed in current opportunities.

Gaps in the framework?

Notice anything missing?

There's no explicit benchmark to highlight the importance of learning about starting or running a business. You could argue that it would be included under Benchmark 8, but you are relying on the skill of the guidance professional, and on the young people identifying this as an interest. The other way in which young people can learn about starting a business is to take business studies at GCSE and/or A level, or undertake a relevant BTEC or apprenticeship.

SMEs are employers of huge numbers of people, yet schools are not *required* to inform young people about how, why or whether to start one. Again, arguably, schools are there to support academic development, but this book is about doing that as well as looking ahead at young people's future careers and places in the world. Some schools link business start-ups to enterprise learning via specific off-timetable days under the PSHEE curriculum. Is this enough? 'Maybe' is the answer – as ever it depends on how the school implements PSHEE and its drop-down/off-timetable/enrichment days, the context in which they are delivered and how the lessons learned are brought back into the classroom.

---

21 Gatsby Charitable Foundation, *Good Career Guidance*, p. 31.

If 5.9 million private businesses exist in the UK and the vast majority (99.3%) have less than 49 employees, it's logical that students are likely to be employed by an SME in the future, as well as there being a chance that they will want to start one.[22] 4.5 million of the private businesses in the UK have no employees – therefore 76% are sole-traders. This could be a neglected part of careers education, but can be overcome by utilising enterprise days or competitions, as well as making sure that the skills of entrepreneurs are investigated and highlighted within careers learning. Lord Young, in his 2014 *Enterprise for All* report, says, 'It is difficult to exaggerate the importance of enterprise in all its forms in a modern economy.'[23] For Lord Young (and me) this needs to start in schools.

What if students' entrepreneurial spark isn't ignited at school and they end up starting their own business because they can't get a 'proper' job? Obviously, this is a cynical view, but it does highlight the accidental nature of learning about enterprise and entrepreneurship, unless your secondary school makes a point of valuing and promoting it. One thing your school could do – as a minimum – is get involved with Global Entrepreneurship Week,[24] which is an initiative held each year during November.

As another aside: the way I found my own purpose in life was realising that the skills and knowledge I'd built up in 17 years doing work for other people had equipped me to deliver business and enterprise workshops in schools to inspire and excite young people. Luckily, at the time I started Innovative Enterprise, there was a huge push (backed by some school-based funding support) by the then Labour government to increase levels of business and enterprise skills in UK schools based on the *Review of Enterprise and the Economy in Education* by Howard Davies in 2002.[25] My finding was quite by accident and the result of me personally being ill-suited to the demands of a full-time job as well as bringing up a young family ... I decided I wanted to 'bring the future to life' for young people as part of their

---

22 Department for Business, Energy and Industrial Strategy, Business Population Estimates for the UK and Regions: 2019 Statistical Release (14 January 2020). Available at: https://www.gov.uk/government/publications/business-population-estimates-2019/business-population-estimates-for-the-uk-and-regions-2019-statistical-release-html.

23 Lord Young, *Enterprise for All: The Relevance of Enterprise in Education* (June 2014), p. 3. Available at: https://assets.publishing.service.gov.uk/government/uploads/system/uploads/attachment_data/file/338749/EnterpriseforAll-lowres-200614.pdf.

24 See https://www.genglobal.org/gew.

25 Howard Davies, *Review of Enterprise and the Economy in Education* (February 2002). Available at: https://www.readyunlimited.com/wp-content/uploads/2011/09/Davies-Review-main-doc.pdf.

school experience rather than them finding out 'by accident' later in life that they could be more enterprising and entrepreneurial.

Another area where careers learning might be falling short is in the arts. A report on the BBC website claims that schools are 'neglecting' the £100-billion arts industry.[26] Art and visual literacy are crucial to the digital and media industries. 'Like reading and writing it [art] has to start from a young age, because only if you understand how an image is made and that you can make your own image, you can understand [the] world,' says Stefan Kalmár from the Institute of Contemporary Arts. In the UK around 64% of those who work as creative or performing artists, authors, journalists or linguists are self-employed,[27] all of whom would have benefitted from learning about business start-ups as a future career option during their time at school.

As well as adopting the Gatsby Benchmarks and starting to measure progress towards them, it is important to consider the culture of the school and how it accommodates future-focus and learning about subjects' future applicability. Culture is crucial to the development of an organisation – how its people operate, what activities take precedence over others, how attitudes are shaped and how targets, aims, goals and missions are achieved. This is especially important in schools with relation to supporting CEIAG, which will blend with academic learning to equip young people to face the world with qualifications, clearly identified skills and confidence.

The careers lead

One of the key roles within an educational setting – if CEIAG is to be introduced, developed, coordinated and sustained – is the careers lead. It's a complex and involved role and one which is supported with qualifications in CEIAG at different levels. In secondary school settings, allocating this responsibility as a part-time role is essential, but as a full-time role is ideal. Working with subject leaders and subject teachers, the careers lead is key to implementing the careers

---

26 *BBC News*, Creative Subjects: The £100bn Industry 'Neglected by Schools' (5 September 2019). Available at: https://www.bbc.co.uk/news/av/uk-england-london-49579764/creative-subjects-the-100bn-industry-neglected-by-schools.
27 Eurostat, Cultural Statistics Report (May 2020), Figure 9. Available at: https://ec.europa.eu/eurostat/statistics-explained/index.php/Culture_statistics_-_cultural_employment#Self-employment.

strategy, making sure that activities are developed and delivered across all subjects and key stages.

The careers lead will also be responsible for coordinating national celebrations related to careers and enterprise activity (NCW, National Apprenticeship Week, Global Entrepreneurship Week, etc.). This person will, typically, coordinate work experience placements and build relationships with local businesses. The future-focus continues with building links to local FE and HE institutions. The careers lead will be key in identifying and promoting open days and finding out if there is funding to support students to travel to local colleges or universities.

The role also includes some elements of data management: coordinating the input of feedback and progress and – if using a tool like Compass+[28] (other commercial careers packages are available) – ensuring data is managed on a regular basis. Remember, data is valuable not only for assessing student outcomes, it is also crucial to justify and reflect SLT budget allocation, governor headline data reports and student outcome reports. It is worth speaking to local organisations such as LEPs, Chambers of Commerce or larger businesses who rely on students as future employees to see if they are willing to support the funding of career toolkits for your young people.[29]

Untapped resources: parents and their workplaces

For a variety of reasons, parents can often be an untapped resource in a school. If a school has a parent–teacher association (PTA) to offer fundraising and administrative support, it should be possible to set up a parent careers association (PCA). The PCA would seek to bring in the expertise and support of parents, open the door to them and their business contacts, and support the students' learning about careers and the world of work in any number of circumstances.

Following the PTA model, the school would ask parents, governors and staff if they would be willing to sit on the PCA for a year, to begin with. Chaired by the head teacher initially and then handed to the

---

28 See https://www.careersandenterprise.co.uk/schools-colleges/compass-plus.
29 'PwC estimate that the total cost of achieving all the benchmarks in a typical school will be equivalent to £54 per pupil from Year 2 onwards.' Gatsby Charitable Foundation, *Good Career Guidance*, p. 39.

careers lead, the meetings would explore options for supporting the school's careers and enterprise plans. Members of the PCA would be asked to commit whatever they could: time, work experience placements, assembly talks, competitions, knowledge, skills, resources, equipment ... whatever they could in return for a DBS check (if required) and the chance to change students' lives.

In areas of low employment and low aspiration (as we saw highlighted by the Careers and Enterprise Company's *Prioritisation Index 2015*), which are affected by intergenerational unemployment and a high number of pupils on free school meals, creating support for parents as part of the PCA could encourage aspiration and learning that would change their lives too. The PCA could also provide help for parents with lower levels of literacy, numeracy, qualification or command of English – for example, classes designed to improve their employability and therefore their appreciation of and support for careers education for their children.

Simply, the PCA could be a vehicle which would benefit all parties locally: students are offered role models, local businesses are linked to the community, and parents are more engaged in their and their children's career prospects. Finally, it could also draw new and enthusiastic people to the school, bringing with them a passion to support careers and enterprise learning. If created as part of a multi-academy trust (MAT) or consortium of local schools and colleges, a PCA would bring many benefits to all concerned.

Conclusion

Every school or college is a community asset with thousands of individual members and dozens of organisational stakeholders. With some planning, some structure from the Gatsby Benchmarks, some funding support and some bravery, that community can pull together to support the education and life chances of the young people at its centre.

It takes a village to raise a child; it takes a community to guide and support them into the future.

Chapter 5

TEACHING TOOLS

Those who are happiest are those who do the most for others.

Booker T. Washington[1]

Subject stepladders: games, tools and resources for every subject

This series of tools, games and exercises are intended to help you start conversations about careers, jobs and the world of work. Not only that, they are intended to make young people question what they have seen of, and heard about, the world of work. This includes challenging assumptions, gathering knowledge of career paths and thinking about the successes (and failures) that define work. These activities can be applied across most subject areas and will also fit into a PSHEE or citizenship curriculum.

Self-reflection task

Think about which subjects first inspired you and made you interested in working within that field. Whether primary or secondary school inspired you, there must have been a point at which you thought, 'This is for me.' What was it, and how can you inspire that thinking in young people today?

---

1 Booker T. Washington, *Up from Slavery: An Autobiography* [Kindle edn] (2015 [1901]), loc. 1255.

STAR of the day

This activity is ideal for form time, perhaps after registration. Using the STAR Model from page 51, ask one student per day (on a rota basis) to stand up and speak about one of their recent achievements. This will develop the habits of self-reflection and self-expression, and plant the idea that we have talents that we need to share for our own self-confidence and to inspire others. It's important to practise overcoming modesty and to become aware that our success isn't just tied to our grades. By doing this in front of peers, others can chip in and highlight the individual's skills from an objective observer's point of view.

Skills watch

Use the 7SAS (see page 35) to assess the skills involved in various jobs – a great way to help students to see the skills inherent in particular fields of work and how they measure up to them. The aim is to build the habit of thinking about skills as well as qualifications, always remembering that students are more than their grades. There are many ways in which you can use the 7SAS. Ideas include:

- As part of a field trip, go and watch people at work and assess their skills according to the 7SAS (e.g. effective oral and written communication 7/10; accessing and analysing information 6/10; initiative and entrepreneurialism 5/10, etc.).

- As a desk exercise, watch careers videos on BBC Bitesize or professional bodies' websites and see which skills are important.

- As an exercise amongst business partners of the school, ask visitors about the skills they use every day during work skills days, for example.

- Watch film or TV clips (e.g. police dramas, soap operas, action films, 'reality' shows, food/house/DIY/travel/wildlife programmes, etc.) and assess different characters, presenters and actors according to their skills.

- National Careers Week Skills Days were launched in May 2020 and are a once-a-term celebration of Skills. See @NCWSkillsDays on Twitter and Instagram.

To put it simply, the 7SAS can and should be used as often as possible to help students see how daily activities demonstrate knowledge of skills. *Just use it!*

10 in a minute

Create quickfire lists of 10 careers/jobs that relate to your subject. Do it once a term and see what changes with time, technological developments, changes in the economy and students' awareness of the world of work. Either get teams of students to create the best list as a competition or get the class to suggest ideas to list on the board, but don't allow repetition. Consider where different subjects overlap in terms of careers – could this be represented as a Venn diagram for more visual impact?

Draw that job

Ask students to do a five-minute drawing of a person working in a specific job: artist, astronaut, author, chef, dentist, doctor, engineer, explorer, farmer, fashion designer, firefighter, musician, newsreader, nurse, paramedic, photographer, pilot, poet, police officer, scientist, teacher, TV host, etc. Once this is complete you can discuss different roles and stereotypes with the class. No one is wrong; we internalise and generalise our experiences. This is a powerful way for primary students, especially, to learn about stereotypes and difference – not just gender but also discrimination along the lines of disability, race, age, etc.[2]

WWW/WWW

What went well/what went wrong? Exploring how fortunate/successful people react when things go wrong is a great way to learn about bouncing back from failure and contingency planning. There are two main lessons to learn from this challenge: firstly, that failure is the chance to start again and, secondly, that people's careers change and

---

2   As we saw in Chambers et al., *Drawing the Future.*

that a 'job for life' is a rare thing. There are a few ways to carry out this activity:

- Watch a documentary about someone famous (e.g. an entrepreneur, scientist, sportsperson, politician, etc.) and see which elements of their lives went well and which didn't go to plan.

- As a teacher, agree to be interviewed by your students about WWW/WWW in your career (discretion required!).

- Get the students to ask other members of staff WWW/WWW.

- Get the students to interview members of the governing body or business visitors.

- Case studies of famous people will nearly always include stories of triumph and tragedy – use them as a way of discussing how plans change and skills develop over time, which leads to new routes.

What's your previous?

Ask teachers, governors and visitors about previous jobs they have done and skills they have built upon during their career journey. This tool from NCW (see page 93), and freely available on the website,[3] is a great way to explore previous experiences and start conversations about different roles and skills that developed from them.

What do they need?

This activity is suitable for primary students or students with SEND. You'll need a set of pictures of people in different types of workwear. They could be photographs of real people or cartoons, but they each need to be wearing outfits related to specific types of work: hard hats, helmets, visors, headsets, different uniforms, high-vis clothing, suits, overalls, etc. If you're creating a set of resources to use again or with different classes, laminate them. Also create a set of pictures of items that they might use – tools, vehicles, equipment, etc. – and then ask the children to match them up.

---

3 See https://nationalcareersweek.com/download/18362/.

WHAT DOES YOUR CAREER PATH LOOK LIKE?

Name:

Previous Jobs:

Skills Developed:

NCW
National Careers Week

#NCW2020

RBS

Tools are available to download from: www.crownhouse.co.uk/featured/the-ladder
This resource is from a wide selection available at: https://ncw2020.co.uk/.

The teacher's role is to ask why the children have matched the prop with the person, and to explore why people in certain jobs use particular equipment. This is good for breaking stereotypes and also for bringing elements like safety and care into the discussion.

As a really fun extension of this activity, you could replace the images with real people (visitors or teachers) and a box of interesting props and/or ask the pupils to get dressed up. Safeguarding needs to be considered if you are inviting visitors in, of course.

Who uses this?

A variation on the preceding activity in which a piece of equipment (or a picture of it) is shown to the class and students have to guess how it is used, who uses it and why. The school could even create a resource box filled with a variety of props brought in by teachers, staff and parents. This could be combined with 20 Questions as a whole-class game show for primary and secondary school usage.

Pathways game show

This is a game for secondary and above to assess knowledge of different pathways and the levels of education needed for each role. The teacher makes sets of four cards, each with one word on: school, college, apprenticeship, university. The students are in teams and the teacher gives them prompts, either by showing a video or picture or reading out the name of a job.

After each prompt, the teams have to hold up the right card to declare what minimum level of qualification is needed for the role. For example:

plumber = college

social worker = university

mechanic = college

entrepreneur = school

You need a good awareness of careers pathways – perhaps link to online resources from your careers system provider or examples from the National Careers Service.[4]

By framing the discussion of pathways into different careers as a fun game, students will engage differently and hopefully be inspired to research careers that are newly on their radar.

Career of the week

An initiative across the school, using either a central careers notice-board on which a different career is highlighted each week, or one in each department. The display could be allocated to students as a research task (which could carry house points or another benefit for the students that get involved) or could be done by a member of staff from each department on a rota basis.

A simple template could be created which includes job name, skills required, subject links, pay and opportunities for travel and advance-ment. Use a picture or two to bring the job to life and possibly a QR code or web link for more information. Slide these into plastic wallets fixed to the walls so that the resources created can be reused.

This can also be used to highlight how careers fit within different subject areas – for example, web designer could fall under IT and art; architect could fall under maths, design technology, art and geography.

Disappearing fast

Students are tasked with creating a list of 10 jobs that have largely disappeared in the past 100 years. They have 10 minutes to do this. Reflect on how the pace of change in terms of technological and industrial developments impacts on employment patterns, and thus on societal structures and social mobility.

Starters for 10 – streetlamp lighters, miners, horse-drawn carriage drivers, tanners, hand spinners. Also reflect that these jobs and skills

---

4   See https://nationalcareers.service.gov.uk.

may be obsolete in some parts of the world but still active in others. Consider too, that some of these skills may have now become 'artisan' crafts and jobs.

Now ask students to make a list of the jobs that are commonplace now that they think will disappear in the next 25 years. This will help to spark debate about the speed of change in the information revolution.

What's my line?

Students are asked to guess the role and industry of a visitor, or group of visitors, to the school. As an interactive session they could be asked a series of up to 20 questions to try and ascertain where they work, who they work with, what training and education they needed, where they studied, which school subjects are important to their role, how often they travel, if they have to wear a special uniform or protective equipment to do their job, etc.

To add to the difficulty/drama, each visitor could be asked to wear a hazmat suit or similar outfit so it's harder to guess from their clothes. To make it more memorable, students could be tasked with writing the jobs they think the person does on their hazmat suit, or on a sticky note which can be pinned on. (NB: the relevant safeguarding guidance needs to be considered here.)

Interview me

Using English and enquiry skills, students are tasked with becoming journalists/reporters to question visitors to the school. This method could be used by primary and secondary schools, varying the expectations of the written reports. The students' articles can be published in the school magazine, as a website story or used as part of the careers library.

These interviews could also be carried out on the telephone or using video technology (e.g. FaceTime, Zoom or Skype). Not only do young people learn how to frame enquiry questions, they also see what it is like to work as a journalist and discover ways to use language creatively. These interviews could, alternatively, be filmed and shared as part of the school careers library – additionally developing students' digital and editing skills.

Would I lie to you?

Three people discuss their careers, but only two of them are telling the truth and one is lying about what they do. After five minutes of questioning the three guests, students have to guess which is which. Using the game show trope of holding up cards (which could be double-sided – 'true' on one side and 'lie' on the other – and laminated for future use) students 'win' by guessing who is telling the truth and who isn't. Each round is followed by information about the careers discussed.

The game could be made more impactful by visitors wearing outfits, bringing in a prop or telling a story. Teachers could also take on the visitor role and talk about their previous jobs.

Career steps

On all the staircases in the school, printed fascias are affixed to the risers, so as pupils climb them they will see the steps needed to get to the careers at the top. Staircases in different parts of the building can be themed – for example, maths and science careers in the science block. You could approach local employers, colleges and universities to sponsor your career steps – and posters which would supply more information on landings and in corridors. Careers posters could include QR codes or web links. Obviously, there are ethical considerations here related to the business of the sponsors and their motives.

As an additional learning tool, students studying art or graphic design could be tasked with creating the graphics for the careers steps.

An example follows, which may need to be adjusted for the educational setting, and, optionally, local needs for the skills and careers and local availability of study – which will clearly depend on local colleges and employers but not necessarily universities.

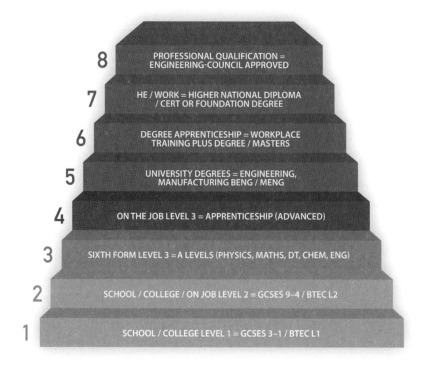

8 — PROFESSIONAL QUALIFICATION = ENGINEERING-COUNCIL APPROVED

7 — HE / WORK = HIGHER NATIONAL DIPLOMA / CERT OR FOUNDATION DEGREE

6 — DEGREE APPRENTICESHIP = WORKPLACE TRAINING PLUS DEGREE / MASTERS

5 — UNIVERSITY DEGREES = ENGINEERING, MANUFACTURING BENG / MENG

4 — ON THE JOB LEVEL 3 = APPRENTICESHIP (ADVANCED)

3 — SIXTH FORM LEVEL 3 = A LEVELS (PHYSICS, MATHS, DT, CHEM, ENG)

2 — SCHOOL / COLLEGE / ON JOB LEVEL 2 = GCSES 9–4 / BTEC L2

1 — SCHOOL / COLLEGE LEVEL 1 = GCSES 3–1 / BTEC L1

As seen here at The Duston School in Northampton, career steps could be accompanied by floor and wall graphics to help students navigate the different subject areas:

Unexpected careers in unexpected places

Here are some ideas for guerrilla career posters and insights in and around the buildings:

- School video display boards – feature the career of the week on them.
- Landings and stairwells – display career boards.
- Changing rooms – who works behind the scenes at sports clubs?
- Reception – what skills do receptionists need and where else do they work?
- School buses and bus stops – who works in transport? Drivers, mechanics, route planners, inspectors, CCTV monitors, disability adaptation designers, etc.
- On computers – who designs these? Who repairs computers? What does a network engineer do? List 10 jobs that use computers.
- Form time job of the day – form tutors read out the information and then display it on the whiteboard before taking the register.
- Canteen – who does what in a kitchen? What skills do chefs have? Tray-top laminated posters about jobs and career routes.
- Playgrounds, bike sheds and sports fields – what do civil engineers do? What skills do groundskeepers need?
- Toilets – a 'careers in the cubicle' poster, which changes monthly, about different careers, job profiles or even information about courses from a local college or university prospectus.

I'm not suggesting that all of these ideas are implemented at the same time across the school. Some of these locations will also be useful for displays of information on other themes – for example, sexual health, bullying, etc. However, once the school is in the habit of sharing information and knowledge about careers it's possible to do this in surprising ways which will surprise, delight and inform students in equal measure, and keep the messages fresh.

This idea was inspired by 'Potty PD' (personal development) at Tring School, where posters are placed in the staff toilets to offer quick hints and tips to teachers about how they can improve their knowledge, practice or skills.

Supplier CSR payback

Business managers in each school or MAT could include a clause in any tenders or works contracts to major suppliers of services – such as catering, architecture, construction, IT supply and fit, accountancy, recruitment consultants, etc. – which compels them to offer some sort of careers input to the school. This could be work experience placements, help with interview skills, or delivering an assembly or careers talk for students, for example. In this way the company will be adding extra value (without significant financial outlay) and offering the students additional insights.

This could also prompt a longer-term relationship between the company and school, which would provide more support for students over a number of years. The company will be able to claim any additional work with the school as a CSR activity, which *may* provide a tax advantage.

Who works here?

Gather a selection of pictures of buildings, venues, places and vehicles and ask who would work here. Link the resources to your subject:

- STEM: airports, factories, garages, etc.
- Arts: the Royal Albert Hall, theatres, museums, galleries, etc.
- Sports: arenas, Olympic parks, golf courses, etc.
- Languages: airports, ports, cruise ships, seaside towns, cities.
- Geography/history: museums, sites of historical significance, palaces, etc.

Challenge students to come up with 10 related jobs at first, then 20, then 30, and then as many as possible. Beyond the obvious – maintenance engineers, cleaners, security, etc. – ask students to think more deeply and more broadly.

The best companies to work for

Use the freely accessible *Sunday Times* Best Companies to Work For list which is published each year to see which are the best large and small companies to work for in the UK.[5]

Use these lists for a number of simple tasks:

- Find out if any of the businesses are local and research them.
- Ask businesses to come in and speak to students.
- Smash stereotypes – e.g. McDonald's was Number 6 in 2017.
- Link companies and industries to subject areas.
- Focus on one company a week to discuss for five minutes in form time.

Higher or lower

This is a comparison exercise involving a number of different job roles – similar to top trumps. Choose a set of criteria to compare – this could be salary, level of qualification needed, length of time to qualify, value of the industry in a particular place, number of people employed in the industry and countries where these roles exist. Create laminated cards featuring your chosen jobs and display them on the board as a timeline or graph. One possible graph could depict the length of learning/qualification time versus the expected salary, for example. The arrangement will give you a visual representation of the variety of different aspects to the careers – learning about investment versus salary; pathways to qualify versus opportunities globally, etc.

As a further element to this game, students can take 10 minutes to research one of the careers in groups and report back to the class. Cautionary note: in rapidly changing times there may be a danger in creating resources about pathways into specific industries – and the salaries that jobs command – as this could change. So make sure you do your research and update your resources regularly – or task this to the students.

---

5   See https://www.b.co.uk/the-lists/.

Subject-specific careers

What follows is a list of jobs and careers connected to different subject areas. These examples show how subjects can be brought to life in relation to students' futures. This can be supported using resources and videos from NCW,[6] BBC Bitesize Careers, data and LMI from the National Careers Service, university departments, colleges, companies, trade associations and a host of other organisations who look to spread messages about working opportunities in their spheres.

Self-reflection task

Before reading on, take a subject – your own or one you enjoyed at school – and, in five minutes, list as many jobs and careers attached (however loosely) to that subject as you can. Try mind-mapping it, it may help.

I'm hoping you get to at least 20 ... go!

Once completed, consider how many of these are roles you've learned about since school and which you would have known about at age 15 or 16.

Try this with your students and see how they get on, see where the gaps are and adjust your examples and links accordingly.

The games and resources in this chapter will help you to consider a number of ways of exploring different careers within and across subject areas. Many of these tools can be used in any subject area with a little adaptation.

- **STEM** – not just a scientist. These subjects lead to work in a number of different and diverse areas: accessibility, analysis, artificial intelligence, audiometrist, automotive/aerospace/transport designer, builder, building surveyor, care home

---

6 https://ncwtv.co.uk/.

manager, carer, chemist, climate change advisor, coder, conservationist, customer and supplier researcher, data manager, dispensing chemist, district nurse, ecological researcher, electrician, engineer (bio, environmental, civil, electrical, electronic, medical, mechanical, nano), environmental developer, health visitor, lab technician, land surveyor, lecturer, manufacturer, medic, nurse, optician, plumber, product designer, product prototyper, product tester, project manager, prosthetic limb designer and 3D printer, quality manager, teacher, telecoms engineer, town planner, vet, welder.

NB: The NHS has over 350 careers available – why not use this resource to help with this exercise: https://www.healthcareers. nhs.uk/.

- **Modern foreign languages (MFL)** – not just a holiday rep. Careers using MFL include: accessibility for all, ambassador, border force worker, British Council worker, companion or advocate, conservationist, corporate guide, diplomatic service roles, financial services roles, global trader, HM revenue and customs roles, international sports roles, manufacturing roles, overseas charity work, overseas legal counsellor, political advisor, teacher, translator, web designer.

- **English** – not only Shakespeare or journalism. Careers could include: accessibility – e.g. Braille translator, comedian, conveyancer, critic, digital designer, EFL tutor, exam invigilator, exam marker, marketing professional, playwright, poet, policy writer, politics roles, printer, proofreader, public relations, quality controller, reader, researcher, script editor/writer, social media expert, solicitor, speech writer, spokesperson, standards assessor, teacher, web content creator/editor, will writer, writer.

- **Food technology/hospitality** – not just a bar person or chef. Careers could include: B&B host, baker, barista, butcher, cookery book developer, food and drink taster, food photographer, food safety advisor/assessor, hotel/bar/pub/coffee shop manager, kitchen/restaurant designer, maître d', meet and greeter, nutritionist (sports and medical), patissier, product developer, recipe tester, restaurant consultant, restaurant reviewer, sommelier, special diets chef, tea blender, travel consultant, travel writer, valet.

- **Art and design** – not just a painter. Careers could include: advertising executive, animator, architect, art therapist, artist, body artist, costume designer, carpenter, crafter, digital designer, documentary maker, exhibition designer, fashion designer, film technician/producer/director, florist, furniture designer, graphic designer, hair and beauty professional, illustrator, industrial designer, interior designer, landscape designer, logo designer, make-up artist, modelmaker, museum and gallery worker, photographer, picture framer, printer, product designer, product prototyper, production designer, sign-maker, special effects artist, sustainable fashion consultant, teacher, textile designer and manufacturer, TV/film set designer, visual merchandiser including point of sale, web designer.

- **Sport** – not just lifeguarding. Careers could include: agent, analyst, anti-doping tester, groundsperson, injury specialist, marketing and PR professional, marketing and sales professional for sports venues, massage therapist, nutritionist, PE teacher, personal trainer, physiotherapist, promotions manager for sportspeople, referee, safety officer, sport club promotor, sport outreach worker, sports doctor/nurse, sports equipment designer, sports equipment promotions manager, sports photographer, sports psychologist, sports reporter, sports scientist, sports scout, sportswear designer, teacher, VAR technologist, youth worker.

- **Music/performing arts** – not all philharmonics. Careers could include: acoustic engineer, actor, advert jingle writer, ambient sound engineer for public venues, busker, composer, digital music technologist, DJ, entertainment lawyer, festival promoter, gig logistics roles, lighting technician, music and sound systems engineer and installer, musician/producer for film and TV, music rights agent, music streaming technologist, music teacher, musician, performance musician, promotional influencer, sound recordist, sound technician, technologist for music, video maker.

- **Geography** – not just colouring in maps. Careers could include: advisor on politics and geography, advisor to governments, agriculturalist, ambassador, British Council, business analyst, courier, diplomat, environmental campaigner, farmer, forces advisor, foreign exchange finance analyst/specialist/trader, foreign office roles, global development consultant, global reporter, global warming expert, human geographer, land agent, lecturer, manufacturing professional, overseas development advisor, population change advisor, secret shopper for travel companies, societal changes analyst, surveyor, sustainable development consultant, teacher, town planner, travel analyst, travel consultant.

- **History** – not just museums. Careers could include: antiques specialist, archaeologist, architectural historian, author, builder, building conservationist, conservation officer, editor, environmental analyst, finance officer, heritage officer, historical expert re: business, insurance analyst, lecturer, political advisor, religious correspondent, researcher, teacher, town planner, tutor.

- **Business** – it's not only accounts. Careers could include: administrator, building and premises manager, business integration engineer, business lawyer, business plan advisor, business systems consultant, business transport and logistics manager, care home manager, communications specialist, consultant, entrepreneur, finance app developer, financial analyst, funding expert, global business analyst/journalist, human resources professional, innovations expert, insurer, investor, IT consultant for businesses, lawyer, market expert, production planner, purchasing manager, report editor, retailer, shop manager, shop owner, sole trader/builder/maintenance expert, solicitor, surveyor, tax advisor, teacher, trademark/intellectual property expert.

Obviously there are hundreds of sub-sections to these jobs – for example, apprentices, trainees, juniors, etc. – and don't forget that many of the jobs in the civilian world will also be repeated in the forces – whether Army, Navy, Royal Air Force or Merchant Navy, they will all need a number of the services above to sustain their work-force, equipment or locations.

Why not suggest that your students add another 10 jobs to each of these lists and maybe even consider which subjects overlap using a Venn diagram or mind map?

Conclusion

These are some simple examples of how you can link careers learning to different subject areas. As technology develops and our working world changes – think about the millions of people world-wide who changed their work patterns and behaviours during the COVID-19 pandemic – different subject areas and skills take on different levels of importance in many roles across all industries. The crucial nature of ICT and languages will have been appreciated when workers needed to join multinational video conference calls and the importance of good grammar and design skills will have been felt during online presentations.

The application of school subjects to the workplace will continue to evolve and the future needs for those subjects will also change. Some subjects will maintain their importance; some will fall by the wayside and others will emerge to take their place.

Regularly undertaking these types of exercises across school subjects will help careers staff and teachers to support broad thinking in subject application and provide up-to-date answers to the oft-asked question: 'Why are we even learning this stuff?'

Chapter 6

CHALLENGING STEREOTYPES: SUPPORT FOR UNDER-REPRESENTATION IN STEM CAREERS

Be so good they can't ignore you.

Steve Martin[1]

Despite the under-representation of a variety of groups of people in different industries and organisations, there are plenty of supportive organisations that want to help schools and colleges to break down barriers for students. The majority of universities have widening participation units to support applications from students who wouldn't usually aspire to HE or believe that it's for them. There is support available from outside organisations to help your practice within school as well as to work directly with students.

'It's hard to be what you can't see,' said Marian Wright Edelman,[2] and under-representation in workplaces, university prospectuses, company brochures and TV advertisements, as well as online and across social media, will contribute to people feeling that they can't aspire to that education/career/lifestyle. In the UK this has been challenged by a number of programmes. Take the under-representation of women in STEM subjects – the following projects and organisations are all working with schools to change the future.

These organisations can support schools in fulfilling the Gatsby Benchmarks on page 76, so I've indicated which benchmarks each example links to. NB: because these examples are external to schools it is difficult to show how these will contribute to Benchmark 1 because that is concerned with a stable careers programme within an educational establishment. The organisations will support schools in terms of their careers programme by offering external experiences and input for their students.

---

1 On the Charlie Rose Show in 2007, Martin was asked about his autobiography *Born Standing Up* – in the answer he said: 'Be so good they can't ignore you.'
2 Marian Wright Edelman, It's Hard to Be What You Can't See, *Children's Defense Fund* [blog] (21 August 2015). Available at: https://www.childrensdefense.org/child-watch-columns/health/2015/its-hard-to-be-what-you-cant-see/.

The Royal Academy of Engineering suggests that the UK will need 124,000 engineers and technicians every year to meet current and future demand for 'core engineering' roles to 2024.[3] Because of this significant requirement, this chapter stands alone in support of STEM-focused careers.

I've included these examples because they are very prominent and/or have won awards, or I have been involved with or know of them through my company's work. In almost all cases they have been started by people who have developed their career despite being under-represented or marginalised in some way.

A Mighty Girl

A Mighty Girl is an online collection of books, toys, films and music for parents, teachers and others who want to support and enable girls to become whatever they want to be. The site has some free resources and posters, and other paid activities and tools to share. Their aim is to equip girls with the competence, confidence and leadership skills to use in whatever life and career direction they choose.

https://www.amightygirl.com

Gatsby Benchmarks: 2 and 4.

Becoming a Doctor

Becoming a Doctor is an initiative started at the University of Manchester medical school by Rajiv Sethi and colleagues to inspire and support young people across the UK to become medical professionals. The team deliver a number of different initiatives for schools and colleges to encourage more young people to consider careers in medicine, mentor them and support their applications. Their aim is widening participation of students from BAME and less-privileged backgrounds. The initiative is free for students and is supported by an annual conference and exhibition at the University of Manchester which puts them in touch with NHS recruiters, employers

3   Royal Academy of Engineering, *Engineering Skills for the Future*, p. 17.

and universities. The initiative also supports interview skills and revision for entrance exams and qualifications.

https://www.becomingadr.org

Gatsby Benchmarks: 2, 3, 4, 5, 7 and 8.

Institute of Civil Engineering

The Institute of Civil Engineering (ICE) has a range of materials and resources to support schools and colleges in delivering careers advice and inspiration. Civil engineers help to design, build and install infrastructure across the world – such as bridges, roads, railways, tunnels: the big structures that make living in the world safe and logistically viable.

ICE resources come in the form of group projects with hands-on activities, presentations and posters, all of which can be delivered by teachers and supported by a team of ICE STEM ambassadors who will engage students in real-world discussions about working as civil engineers. Ambassadors are likely to come to schools which are proximal to their workplace, so they are likely to be able to share knowledge of local opportunities and pathways.

https://www.ice.org.uk/what-is-civil-engineering/inspire-the-next-generation/educational-resources

Gatsby Benchmarks: 2, 4, 5, 6 and 8.

Science Grrl

Science Grrl was born in 2012 after a promotional video called 'Science: It's a Girl Thing' was launched to (supposedly) support more women into STEM careers. Sadly, the video contained no actual science and instead offered all the stereotypical 'science lady' tropes of girls looking over the top of their glasses and wearing white lab coats. After a Twitter storm of derision, a group of scientists got together to create Science Grrl to promote a more up-to-date agenda and actually support young women into STEM careers.

Example events include live lectures from Professor Brian Cox, events at science and industry museums at which female scientists discuss their work, and regional networking groups which connect women, employers and educators.

Science Grrl's *Through Both Eyes* research report highlights that 'the percentage of female A-level physics students has hovered at around 20% for the past 20 years',[4] so it's no wonder that leadership roles in STEM companies are hugely male-dominated and will continue to be if things don't change.[5] The UK also 'boasts' the 'lowest proportion of female engineers in the EU'.[6] The report calls on the government, academics, educators, the STEM community and retailers – with their range of toys and clothing – to address how science is seen and promoted because of the need 'to embed gender equality and broader inclusion issues into better STEM education and careers advice for everyone'.[7]

www.sciencegrrl.co.uk

Gatsby Benchmarks: 2, 3, 4, 5, 6 and 7.

Stemettes

Stemettes was started by Anne-Marie Imafidon, MBE, to inspire girls and young women aged 5–22 to consider STEM subjects and careers through school-based activities, CSR visits to companies and mentoring.

Their vision is to ensure that 'All girls will be able to make informed decisions about careers in Science, Technology, Engineering and Maths (STEM), so that eventually women can be proportionally repre-sented in the field. So that we can have 30%+ of the UK's STEM workforce being female, as opposed to just 21%.'[8]

Dr Imafidon set up Stemettes after attending the Grace Hopper Celebration of Women in Computing – a series of awards – in 2012

---

4 Anna Zecharia, Ellie Cosgrave, Liz Thomas and Rob Jones, *Through Both Eyes: The Case for a Gender Lens in STEM* (2014), p. 4. Available at: https://sciencegrrl.co.uk/assets/ SCIENCE-GRRL-Stem-Report_FINAL_WEBLINKS-1.pdf.
5 Zecharia et al., *Through Both Eyes*, p. 7.
6 Zecharia et al., *Through Both Eyes*, p. 4.
7 Zecharia et al., *Through Both Eyes*, p. 5.
8 See https://stemettes.org/about-us/.

and reflecting that she had been one of only three women in a class of 70 when she was at university. Later she attended a Spotlight on STEM event from Business in the Community[9] (the Prince of Wales' responsible business network) and heard about the dearth of women in STEM fields. She decided to do something about it and since her creation of Stemettes nearly 45,000 young women and girls have attended one of their events and 95% are now more interested in STEM subjects.[10] Stemettes partners with organisations like Merrill Lynch, KPMG, Ford, Microsoft, Bloomberg, BT and BP amongst many others.

Dr Imafidon has also founded a scholarship funded by technology organisations to support women to study computing subjects at Durham University.

www.stemettes.org

Gatsby Benchmarks: 2, 3, 4, 5 and 8.

Tomorrow's Engineers

Tomorrow's Engineers harnesses the power of the engineering community in the UK to inspire and educate young people about engineering careers and opportunities. Tomorrow's Engineers is a collaborative initiative which pools the knowledge and skills of the engineering bodies and companies involved and supports young people to develop awareness of and enthusiasm for STEM subjects and careers.

Volunteers work on a number of designated challenges or workshops in schools to make a difference to young people's vision of engineering careers. The country and economy need more engineers and Tomorrow's Engineers' volunteers managed to work with 300,000 young people in one year.[11] That's a big reach and in the long run they are making a difference.

They host a number of events. Big Bang engineering fairs take place in large exhibition venues and aim to inspire thousands of children and teachers at once. Tomorrow's Engineers Week provides hands-on

---

9   See https://www.bitc.org.uk/who-we-are/.
10 See https://stemettes.org/about-us/.
11 See https://www.tomorrowsengineers.org.uk/about-us/overview/.

activities and celebrations of engineering careers, supported by organisations, universities and colleges.

Resources are available for teachers and young people to learn more about engineering, pathways into careers, and the skills required and how to develop them. Annually, during Tomorrow's Engineers Week, The Big Assembly – an event which allows schools to celebrate engineering – is broadcast into school halls, theatres and classrooms across the UK to inspire young people to become more curious about engineering. Their careers resources page for educators is excellent.

https://www.tomorrowsengineers.org.uk

Gatsby Benchmarks: 2, 3, 4, 5, 7 and 8.

Women into Manufacturing and Engineering (WiME)

WiME is an excellent regional initiative pioneered by Dr Kirsty Klode in Hull as a way of encouraging more women and girls into STEM careers. The reason why Hull and the Humber region has been chosen for this initiative is its recent ambition to become an 'Energy Estuary'.[12] With new environmental manufacturing developments in the region – anchored by the Siemens Gamesa wind turbine plant – the Humber region benefits from 17% of its employment being in manufacturing (against around 8.7% nationally).[13] However, there is still a significant under-representation of women in this industry. The aim is to dramatically increase the number of women in STEM careers in the region and a concerted effort is being undertaken by partners Siemens Gamesa, Green Port Hull, Airco and Job Centre Plus, via schools, colleges and the University of Hull, to make this happen. This is an excellent example of a regional demand being satisfied in an innovative way using CSR and targeted careers advice.

Is there something similar being championed for your region?

https://greenporthull.co.uk/jobs-training/women-into-manufacturing-and-engineering

Gatsby Benchmarks: 2, 3, 4, 5, 6, 7 and 8.

---

12 Hull LEP, The Humber's Blueprint for an Industrial Strategy (2018). Available at: https://www.humberlep.org/wp-content/uploads/2018/06/The-Humbers-Blueprint.pdf.
13 See https://greenporthull.co.uk/jobs-training/women-into-manufacturing-and-engineering.

Conclusion

These schemes support women and under-represented groups into careers involving STEM subjects. The Royal Academy of Engineering report into the UK STEM education landscape found that there were more than 600 organisations operating in this field.[14] It is recommended that school careers leads discuss their requirements with LEP representatives, contact local businesses directly (with specific ideas that they want to discuss), ask other local schools for recommendations and consult other teachers via Twitter or forums on the Science Association website.[15]

There are dozens more schemes which work to support young people from all backgrounds in all types of school – some are businesses, some charities, some CICs – and they provide careers experience, workshops, insights, talks and activities. The descriptions, discussions and links to these and other programmes and resources are highlighted in Chapter 7.

All CSR projects respond to a given need at a particular time – I want these projects to inspire reflection in teachers and careers leads and to promote the idea of connecting with businesses and outside organisations. Organisations which are local to you may already be running similar schemes – if not, please use these ideas to promote debate and open the possibility of further outreach work to support your students. Remember also that this work can benefit the collaborating organisation and its staff as well as your students and staff.

14 Royal Academy of Engineering, *Engineering Skills for the Future*, p. 31.
15 See https://www.britishscienceassociation.org.

Chapter 7

RESOURCES, PROGRAMMES, SUPPORT AND LINKS

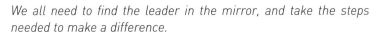

We all need to find the leader in the mirror, and take the steps needed to make a difference.

Arianna Huffington[1]

Who can help us?

Alongside the tools embedded in the CASK in Chapter 2 and the resources in Chapter 5, the following recommendations are for you to use to support students and/or provide activities to complement your teaching. They may also help you to engage governors and inspire local employers to support your school by giving them ideas about how to use their CSR budget and time allocation to benefit students.

This chapter contains a number of links to industry, education, third sector, careers and volunteering organisations that may be helpful to students and teachers, and some case studies for you to use for ideas and reference.

Some of the organisations featured support schools with thinking about the future by offering careers inspiration, workshops and work experience. Again, some have been nominated for or have won awards; some I've worked alongside.

Please remember to consider the 7SAS from the CASK when you're looking at each of the projects – different projects will affect and support your students, staff and partners in different ways and will contribute to enhancing and supporting a variety of developing skills.

---

1   Arianna Huffington, *Thrive: The Third Metric to Redefining Success and Creating a Happier Life* (London: WH Allen, 2014), p. 224.

Each of the examples and case studies included here has been linked to the Gatsby Benchmarks. The majority of the cases won't show any links to Benchmark 1 – a stable careers programme – mainly because this has to be created by the educational establishment themselves. Obviously, forming links to programmes like these will contribute to Benchmark 1, but I can't score it as such – only the setting itself can do that.

BBC Bitesize Careers

As mentioned previously, this is a great repository of short videos (around two minutes long) of people exploring their careers. They are searchable by school subject and include information about next steps (apprenticeships, FE or HE), job profiles and tips and support for the application process. Free to use and great for different and up-to-date perspectives on the world of work. Perfect as a form-time activity or to help link subjects to future careers.

https://www.bbc.co.uk/bitesize/careers

Gatsby Benchmarks: 2, 4, 5, 6 and 7.

The Dame Kelly Holmes Trust

The Dame Kelly Holmes Trust was set up in 2008 by Olympic gold medallist Kelly Holmes to support 11–25-year-olds who are harder to engage in both education and the community. Programmes are delivered by top athletes, often former Olympians, and aim to help some of the hardest to reach young people in the UK.

Programmes boost young people's confidence, resilience and self-esteem through mentoring and sporting activities to support them to move into employment, become community leaders and improve their educational outcomes and well-being.

The trust is particular about the young people who can join the scheme. It was set up to provide maximum support for those who need it most: young people who don't have the confidence or self-esteem to achieve their potential.

The young people accepted onto the scheme have to overcome a number of significant challenges in their personal, home or educational lives; the support from a trusted and inspirational adult can be the guiding hand that they need. Since the London 2012 Olympics the trust has transformed the lives of thousands of young people who are facing disadvantage.

https://www.damekellyholmestrust.org

Gatsby Benchmarks: 3, 4, 5, 6 and 8.

Dream Placement Scheme:
Centre for Leadership Performance

Since 2012 the Centre for Leadership Performance has run the Dream Placement programme in Cumbria. A rural and sparsely populated county, there have traditionally been few employment opportunities there – linked to heavy industry in Barrow, Carlisle, Workington and at the Sellafield nuclear site – but few other options. A historical lack of HE in the county also led to young people moving away for university and not coming back.

In an effort to stop this brain drain and to help harness the skills and minds of local young people, the Dream Placement began as a funded partnership between a couple of dozen employers and local schools.

It is a comprehensive programme of high-level work experience for Years 12 and 13 (students aged 17–18). They work alongside senior leaders and directors in different businesses across the county, gaining experience on projects, participating in meetings and travelling to work sites across the UK. Dream Placement is a great example of a programme designed to answer a specific *local* challenge for young people and employers.

https://dreamplacement.org.uk/noticeboard

Gatsby Benchmarks: 2, 3, 4, 5, 6 and 8.

(In the interests of disclosure, I designed the materials for the Dream Placement and deliver development and recruitment days.)

FabLab Warrington

FabLab Warrington was started in 2016 to offer a creative space which inspires and educates entrepreneurs, artists and makers on their creative journey. It takes its lead from the Fabrication Lab concept pioneered by the Grassroots Invention Group at the Massachusetts Institute of Technology (MIT) in 2001. FabLab is based at Beamont Collegiate Academy in Warrington and grew from the passion of one of the teaching staff into a true education and industry partnership.

FabLab is comprised of a team of professional designers, creatives and technicians with expert machinery, including for 3D design and printing, manufacture and conceptualisation. Masterclasses in coding and engineering, and partnerships with local businesses, ensure that STEM learning is designed into everything they do.

A recent partnership with United Utilities, a regional water and power provider in the north-west, has seen FabLab win a national STEM award for a project involving students from four local academies. A legacy of the project is that 45% of the students involved said that they were more interested in a STEM-related career after being involved in the project.[2]

FabLab used their equipment and skills to 3D print and manufacture face shields for NHS staff during the COVID-19 outbreak. Students whose parents were key workers remained in school to support this innovative manufacturing mission.

http://fablab.warrington.ac.uk

Gatsby Benchmarks: 2, 3, 4, 5, 6, 7 and 8.

Future First

Much has been written about the power and value of alumni networks; American universities use them not only as inspiration but also as a major source of donations. In the UK, alumni associations at universities are smaller, less geared around fundraising and more focused on influence and aspiration. UK independent schools have well-established alumni associations; however, in the state sector

---

2   See http://fablab.warrington.ac.uk/united-utilites-project.html.

alumni associations are – if not unheard of – few and far between. Future First is a UK charity which supports social mobility and aims to increase the number of state school alumni networks.

Harking back to the Edelman quote in Chapter 6, for almost 50% of pupils from the poorest backgrounds– those who qualify for free school meals – their view of success and self-worth is adversely affected because they don't know a single person in the job they want to do in future.[3] Future First wants to see every state school and college in the UK supported by a thriving and enthusiastic alumni community.

https://futurefirst.org.uk

Gatsby Benchmarks: 2, 3, 4, 5 and 7.

Generation Medics

Generation Medics was set up in 2013 to raise awareness of careers in medicine. Many pupils from disadvantaged backgrounds don't believe they have what it takes to make it in medicine or healthcare. Generation Medics works with thousands of volunteers to deliver experiences in schools that raise awareness of healthcare careers.

The volunteers from a variety of medical professions bring a pop-up hospital into schools to allow students to get hands-on with tools and equipment as well as opening up discussions about jobs, careers and pathways into various roles in the NHS. Discussions with practising professionals allow students to see that whatever their backgrounds and current aspirations, there are ways to open the doors into the medical profession.

https://generationmedics.org.uk

Gatsby Benchmarks: 2, 3, 4, 5, 6, 7 and 8.

---

3   See https://futurefirst.org.uk/our-purpose/.

Greenhouse Sports

Greenhouse Sports is a charity built on the idea that sport can develop young people's social, thinking, emotional and physical (STEP) abilities. Greenhouse Sports works with young people from disadvantaged backgrounds to ensure their vision that 'every child has a fair chance to succeed' is realised: 68% of the participants are from postcodes classed as 'high deprivation' by the government. There are around 50 programmes working across London schools to ensure that more students reach the recommended weekly physical activity levels – currently only 16% do.[4]

The research backing Greenhouse Sports' activity shows that sport increases social integration, supports mental health (87% of young people on their programmes had improved their confidence),[5] reduces obesity rates and increases attentiveness and attendance in class.[6]

Sports clubs are delivered at the school premises by professional coaches. Alongside tuition in sport, one-to-one mentoring sessions are available to participants, which support involvement in sporting and learning opportunities outside and inside school. In 2018/19 57,000 hours of coaching and mentoring were delivered in schools by Greenhouse Sports teams.[7]

www.greenhousesports.org

Gatsby Benchmarks: 2, 3, 4, 5 and 8.

Innovative Enterprise

Since 2006 Innovative Enterprise (IE) has designed and delivered workshops for more than 150,000 people in schools, colleges and universities in the careers and enterprise, PSHEE and citizenship curriculum areas as well as working with businesses across the UK. IE's Enterprise Soapbox began life as a kit allowing schools to design,

---

4   Greenhouse Sports, Annual Review 2018–19 (2019), p. 10. Available at: https://www.greenhousesports.org/wp-content/uploads/2019/12/Greenhouse-Sports-Annual-Review-2018-19-Final.pdf.
5   Greenhouse Sports, Annual Review 2018–19, p. 17.
6   Greenhouse Sports, Annual Review 2018–19, pp. 10–11.
7   Greenhouse Sports, Annual Review 2018–19, p. 16.

make, brand and sell soap products according to a UK- and EU-approved cosmetics recipe and evolved into a popular workshop which links enterprise, careers, entrepreneurship, design and creativity.

Stock Market Challenge is a workshop and online simulation of the stock market trading floor and teaches about enterprise, teamwork and risk versus responsibility. It brings maths and communication skills to the fore.

IE has partnered with the Manufacturing Institute's Make It challenges since 2008, designing and delivering STEM-based challenges with Year 9 and 10 students across the UK and UAE.

https://innovativeenterprise.co.uk

Gatsby Benchmarks: 2, 3, 4, 5, 6, 7 and 8.

Job Swap: Brother UK

Senior executives at Brother UK – the UK arm of the global electronics giant – perform a job-swap initiative in which senior executives and leaders of the organisation swap roles with apprentices across the business for a day. Here, in his own words, is why managing director Phil Jones, MBE, has created this amazing project and delivers it annually.

Case study: Brother UK

When I was young, the prospect of one day becoming managing director of a large company would have seemed an impossibility. Low on confidence and self-esteem, not particularly academic, from a single parent family on a council estate – all the indicators would normally predict a different outcome for someone in my demographic.

My prospects, outlook and confidence all began to improve when I entered work and eventually – in 2013, after 20 years with the company – I walked through our front door as managing director, against all the odds.

It led me to become passionate about ensuring that we too provide opportunities for young people with similar backstories. Alongside work experience and career counselling for those still at school, we do our job swap annually, in which senior executives swap roles with apprentices for the day.

Providing a real-life experience of what it takes to run a company, to manage a complex workload and to make big decisions, it can initially scare the pants off a young person but by the end of the day they get a real sense of what it takes and how they could build up their experience to get there one day.

It takes some planning to ensure that the multiple scenarios I leave for them to consider are relevant and challenging, all things that are – in reality – part of the job. The reward comes in seeing the individuals involved get to the end of the day with a sense of achievement and new-found confidence in their ability. A spark which we hope will fan a future flame of ambition.

Phil Jones, MBE, Managing Director, Brother UK

https://brother.co.uk

Gatsby Benchmarks: 3, 5, 6 and 8.

Make It

Created in 2008, the Manufacturing Institute's Make It campaign was created to inspire young people to consider careers in manufacturing. The project was originally funded by the (now closed) Northwest Regional Development Agency as a way of promoting the huge variety of manufacturing businesses across the north-west of England.

The format is a regional competition in which teams of Year 9 students compete in heats sponsored by local manufacturers, with the top 12–18 teams competing in the grand final at an important regional venue – examples have included Old Trafford and the Science and Industry Museum. Year 9 is chosen as the target age, in the hope that the challenge will help them to consider STEM subjects when they choose their options.

Each challenge follows a similar format with students being given different realistic job titles and working together to develop a new product or service based on the sponsoring company's products (examples have included search and rescue vehicles, new food products and electronic devices to combat climate change).

Alongside creating a new product and improving their skills, the young people involved have the chance to meet employees and apprentices from the businesses, discuss career paths and also be involved in a realistic business simulation, culminating in a pitch to senior team members in front of around 100 people.

Some statistics from Make It:

- Annual average engagement since 2008 = 946 Year 9 pupils.
- 134 teachers.
- 153 manufacturing partner volunteers.
- 98% of teachers say that Make It improves students' perceptions of manufacturing, and following Make It would promote it to students on their return to school as their perceptions had also changed.

Twitter: @MakeItUK

Gatsby Benchmarks: 2, 3, 4, 5, 6, 7 and 8.

National Careers Service

The National Careers Service is funded and administered by the government in Westminster and is a tool for anyone living in England who is looking to research the working world or develop their career. The website contains reams of LMI, which is searchable in many ways. Starting with the industry of interest, the site lists the types of careers available, what they look like, the roles and pathways available and the qualifications needed. Overviews of day-to-day tasks are then topped off with salaries, hours of work and the skills needed to undertake the role.

The National Careers Service is free to access and can be a great way to assess the bare bones of a career or job. It's also great for parents to help their children with careers understanding and to plan possible routes to future learning, training and careers.

All the nations in the UK have their own versions of the National Careers Service.

https://nationalcareers.service.gov.uk (England)

https://www.myworldofwork.co.uk (Scotland)

https://careerswales.gov.wales (Wales)

https://www.nidirect.gov.uk/campaigns/careers (Northern Ireland)

Gatsby Benchmarks: 2, 3, 4, 7 and 8.

National Careers Week

NCW started in 2011 when Nick Newman (who we met in Chapter 1) – after more than a decade in careers education – became so frustrated with government changes to the funding of careers education that he felt he had to do something positive to boost its profile. NCW started on Twitter (as the #SaveCareers campaign) as a way for educators to share their expertise and experiences in delivering careers education: they documented how they had developed partnerships and what their students were learning through their activities.

Now NCW (distinct from the National Careers Service) generally falls in the first full week of March each year and is a week-long celebration (and a great incentive/excuse to do something in every educational establishment) of CEIAG. NCW is *always* free for schools, colleges and universities to access as it is funded through sponsorship from large employers and niche industry organisations and providers of careers support and education.

Free resources, guides, games, graphics, posters and competitions are created and made available through the website. During the week different sponsors take hold of the social media feeds and share content using the hashtag NCW followed by the year (e.g. #NCW2021).

This guided organic approach means the reach is huge compared to the budget spent on marketing (which is virtually zero), largely because those that engage with NCW are able to share their expertise as well as gather ideas and enthusiasm from others in the field. Recent useful tools have included NCW guides for governors, Ofsted inspection frameworks and primary careers resources. 2020 saw the launch of an NCW video channel[8] with syndicated content from various providers including the BBC, NatWest Group and various other large organisations.

https://nationalcareersweek.com

Gatsby Benchmarks: 2, 3, 4, 5, 6, 7 and 8.

(In the interests of disclosure, I – along with four others – am a director of NCW CIC).

Queensberry Alternative Provision

Queensberry Alternative Provision is a charity set up to support young people in the north-west of England. At the time, the number of permanent exclusions in Cheshire schools was rising, with these excluded young people likely to become another statistic by joining the 763,000 16–24-year-olds classed as NEETs in the UK.[9]

Queensberry Alternative Provision is based on boxing skills linked to mentoring and support for pupils at risk of exclusion from secondary school. It has been funded by the National Lottery and links closely with the police and prison service.

Programmes are related to numeracy and literacy and include a number of support measures to keep students in mainstream school and prevent them from turning to crime, alongside increasing their employability and life skills.

https://www.queensberryap.com

Gatsby Benchmarks: 2, 3, 4, 5 and 8.

---

8   See https://ncwtv.co.uk/.
9   Office for National Statistics, Young People Not in Education, Employment or Training [statistical bulletin] (27 February 2020). Available at: https://www.ons.gov.uk/employmentandlabourmarket/peoplenotinwork/unemployment/bulletins/youngpeoplenotineducationemploymentortrainingneet/february2020.

STEM Learning

STEM Learning wants to make sure that world-leading STEM education is delivered to all young people across the UK though a number of avenues:

• Teacher CPD, awards and development courses.

• Inspiring groups and communities using STEM ambassadors.

• Engaging employers and industries to support schools and colleges.

STEM Learning is based in York and its initiatives work to link employers with primary, secondary, FE and HE providers to facilitate access to support, ambassadors and resources. The aim is to bring STEM learning to life and therefore promote STEM career opportunities.

https://www.stem.org.uk

Gatsby Benchmarks: 2, 3, 4, 5, 6, 7 and 8.

The Talent Foundry

The Talent Foundry (formerly the Transformation Trust) works with the UK's most challenged secondary schools. Along with their corporate partners – including Barclays, Dell and M&G/Prudential – they provide experiences to raise the awareness and aspiration of students who have had fewer life opportunities. In their first decade the organisation worked with more than 1,600 state schools and more than 600,000 students, offering 2.9 million hours of employability training.[10]

CEO Amy Leonard started the project after a successful corporate career when she realised, on her commute through the Isle of Dogs in London's East End, that very little of the wealth and benefits of the City and Canary Wharf were enjoyed by local families.

Amy jumped out of corporate life, set up the trust as a charity and used her connections to gather funding to create supportive programmes

---

10 See http://talentfoundry.org.uk/About-Us/.

for schools based on the business skills students would need in the future.

Case study: The Talent Foundry

Schools offer a range of opportunities for students of all ages, but for secondary schools an employability scheme creates a bridge between the world of the teenager and the world of the adult. A good employability scheme provides five key areas of development to help a young person develop into a young adult: experience, confidence, knowledge, maturity and alternatives. Avoiding buzzwords or psychobabble, these five areas can, and will, be developed in the curriculum and pastoral support of many schools; however, an employability programme delivers them in a more direct form.

The experience of visiting a workplace – or having employers visit your school – widens the perspective of many students, whose view of the world of work is otherwise limited to what they learn from family and friends. The direct experience of doing work-related activities engages and applies skills they may not consider using or enjoying within the confines of the curriculum. The confidence gained from this experience and the opportunity to practise skills in a safe non-school environment provides more than one step towards adulthood and the world of work. Repeat visits to this world via an employability scheme help to demystify the working world and allow students to navigate their post-school life with greater self-belief.

For many schools without a range of careers provision, an employability scheme offers students and staff knowledge of different professions. Students don't all fit a particular mould and don't have the knowledge to judge what they might want to do from the large number of different jobs out there. The more students are exposed to different roles within organisations, the more they will be in a position to make positive, informed choices about career pathways and, therefore, more educated choices about the qualifications or routes they'll need to take.

You need a level of autonomy and confidence to apply your skills in the world of work. The maturity gained from practising skills within an employability scheme gives students the chance to engage with adults on a more equal footing, completing activities that replicate real-world working scenarios and viewing themselves not as students but as prospective employees.

Finally, an employability scheme offers an alternative. The perception of success for many students is rooted in exams and HE, a direct line that runs from school through university and on to the destination of a 'great' job. The reality that most adults acknowledge is that the route to their current employment was not straightforward, and included different roles in different organisations, the success and failure of job applications, additional training courses and many ups and downs. The employability scheme shows this and suggests some alternatives that young people may not have considered. The best schemes provide students with the opportunity to decide what they don't want, as well as what they do.

Amy Leonard, MBE, CEO, The Talent Foundry

One of the employability programmes delivered by The Talent Foundry, in partnership with Dell, is Powering Transformations, which tasks students with creating a digital tool to support the community. It could be a smartphone app, a public information system or a way of getting the community to work together to overcome a challenge. The programme is delivered by The Talent Foundry at universities across the UK, supported by staff volunteer mentors from Dell. It's not just the young people who benefit from the programme.

http://talentfoundry.org.uk

Gatsby Benchmarks: 2, 3, 4, 5 and 8.

W Communications

W Communications, a public relations (PR) agency in central London, was noticing a dearth of diversity in applicants and employees (caused, they realised, by a lack of social mobility) and so chose a different and radical route to finding and supporting young talent: a programme they have called WX.

WX is a social enterprise which offers three-month paid internships to five young people aged between 18 and 21 who have basic education (GCSE or equivalent) at a time. Warren Johnson, who founded W Communications with Zoe Stafford, said, 'there is a huge pool of talent out there that is being overlooked' … 'we want to give our trainees a really interesting, formative experience that inducts them through every aspect of PR.'[11] The interns will work on real creative briefs. 'They already have those in-built skills – even if they don't realise it – that clients and brands are looking for', said Johnson.

Social mobility through social enterprise. I like it.

https://www.wxcommunications.co.uk

Gatsby Benchmarks: 2, 3, 5, 6 and 8.

Conclusion

The intention of this chapter has been to share best practice examples of how businesses, corporations and charities have worked with education establishments to support teachers and young people by offering careers education programmes and bringing skills and work to life.

Take these project outlines and case studies as impetus to seek out and connect with local or national businesses and charities who may be offering this kind of support, or even as inspiration to approach local organisations to see if they can offer something similar.

Some say that there is nothing new under the sun, but 'new' is relative. It may mean the application of a new project in your school or college, new careers opened up to your students or new ideas about how to engage your students in work-based learning.

Make new happen in your setting using these examples. After all, careers inspiration has to start somewhere.

---

11 Quoted in Hickman, W Launches Social Enterprise to 'Fundamentally Change' Industry's Talent Pipeline.

Chapter 8

SUPPORTING STUDENTS WITH SPECIAL EDUCATIONAL NEEDS AND DISABILITIES WITH THEIR CAREER ASPIRATIONS

The truth is that the story we tell about our life becomes the story of our life.

James Kerr[1]

The aim in this chapter is to offer the view from people who support those with learning difficulties or disabilities, and those in special schools, about how their careers offering helps their young people to aspire and grow. The case studies included here, written by professionals in the SEND sphere, will hopefully provide inspiration and ideas for teachers who are looking for ways to challenge stereotypes and bring more diversity into their classrooms, and want to engage employers' help.

Flip the narrative: Elly Chapple

Elly Chapple is a disability campaigner and advocate. Inspired by the challenges faced by her daughter, Ella, who is deafblind, Elly campaigns to engage everyone in identifying and supporting what people can do, instead of what they can't. Her website features blogs, stories and her TEDx Talk, and she uses #flipthenarrative on social media.[2]

---

1 James Kerr, *Legacy: What the All Blacks Can Teach Us about the Business of Life* (London: Constable, 2013), p. 91.
2 See https://candoella.com/.

Case study: how do we flip the narrative around the work–life pathway?

There is a whole world out there. One we can access and be within. But what if you find yourself within the part of society that we still deem 'different'? I say we, but I know many of us do not see that difference and find ourselves working constantly to change the view. There is still much to be done to create equality for all, and this is an attempt to look at things through a different lens.

I once heard a group of professionals, at a conference, discussing a deafblind child who had expressed that they would like to be an astronaut when they grew up. The discussion was about how to let this student know that it was an impossibility. I was really saddened that the people this child might rely on for help in working towards their life goals or future dreams couldn't accept that they had expressed a desire and that it was valid. This is human and something all children do. Becoming an astronaut is – admittedly – unlikely, but to aim for such a goal, students need to be equipped with skills: being able to read, communicate, achieve – the list is endless. To diminish the goal, to me, was a reductive response. It made me think more about why the adults were so afraid to try, afraid to aim high or believe in the student.

When we think about education, we often think of longer-term goals and aspirations – we use those words when looking at education, health and care plans (EHCPs) and I often wonder, for many, how far we can look ahead at careers, especially with so many struggling to gain an education first, within a system that is not equal for all. Are we really serious about the long-term goals of all young people? Are we paying lip service to inclusion whilst denying some young people the pathways to pursue their needs and wants? Do we understand that by not investing in the education of all, and believing in the ability of all, we are creating problems for future generations who could contribute to society and would like to – given an equal chance – aspire to something that many of us take for granted?

The ability to be independent, to have value in the world outside of the school walls, and to have our own money are just some of the things that perhaps we all take for granted in our daily lives. What if your access to those things is impeded by the fact that society is not yet geared up to allow everyone equal participation? What if you have a visual impairment or a mobility need that means you find it difficult to make your way through life? Or other differences which mean you need support or adjustments to make things accessible and possible – human even – and for you to be in the world like anyone else?

There are numerous people who speak expertly about the world of careers and disability – and I would not attempt to match those voices. Suffice it to say, I would recommend – if you are interested in the 'how to' – that you look at the work being done by Genius Within[3] and Disability Rights UK,[4] and it is worth everyone, especially employers and schools, revising their understanding of the Equality Act 2010.[5] It's also worth *all* of us remembering that disability is one of the few diversity groups which any of us might become a member of, with 80% of disabilities being acquired between the ages of 18 and 64 – the workforce age.[6]

My daughter is deafblind and has other things to contend with. I often wonder what she will do in terms of a career, how it will happen and what will be possible. I don't speculate about the future often because we have a lot to do in the present and that is where she remains daily. The future will be what it is because she has critical jobs to get through first: like learning to read and, eventually, to be independent with her lack of vision, to manage her anxiety (that is a fine daily balancing act in our unforgiving world) and to cope with her health, which can stop her in her tracks. We also have the annual review of her education to manage, which means preparing to demonstrate her right to the education and support she receives, to begin to work towards attaining future goals. Imagine, if you will, every child in the country having to defend their value and prove that they are worthy of

---

3   See https://www.geniuswithin.co.uk/employment-support/.
4   See https://www.disabilityrightsuk.org/access-work.
5   See https://www.equalityhumanrights.com/en/equality-act-2010/what-equality-act.
6   See https://www.weforum.org/agenda/2019/04/what-companies-gain-including-persons-disabilities-inclusion/.

support to gain an education and some independence. There would be uproar. Consider it like this:

---

if we describe some children as having special educational *needs*, not *rights*, then there is also a sense that meeting that need is optional. If we agree that non-disabled children have a right to their education then so should disabled children, regardless of whether or not some, or all, of that education is labelled as 'special'. Education is a right for all. Education is not a chocolate biscuit.[7]

So why, I wonder – perhaps naively – do we allow the void of difference to grow? Surely humans should support one another to reach similar goals – goals that are not gold medals, but enable you to live in the world like anyone else. Perhaps there is still a view that it's a 'nice to have', when in reality it's a human right, as Katherine Runswick-Cole so eloquently explains.

If you are reading this you might be wondering what you can do to help provide future pathways and careers for young people with SEND, if they so wish. The advice I have is human and simple, coming from our experience. My daughter needed people to believe in her for a start. She needed to know that people had high expectations of what she can do in life, rather than only seeing what she can't. Working *with* students imbues a real sense of authenticity about the goal you're working towards together. It's not tokenistic; it's saying, 'I will walk with you and we will find a way through', and really meaning that. Belief in someone transfers across, however you might try to hide it. So, if you find yourself struggling with the 'how' and the 'why', you need to ask for help yourself, because the student will be aware. Within Ella's care team we reflect daily on what we could do better to enhance our understanding of what she needs to get to her goal, and we ask her often if we have got it right.

Doing to, or for, students creates a sense of dependency and a removal of choice. If you consistently do something for or to

---

7   Katherine Runswick-Cole, Education is not a Chocolate Biscuit. In Emma McGarry and Adam J. B. Walker (eds), *Special Rights* (London: Serpentine Galleries, 2018), pp. 13–15 at p. 15. Available at: https://www.serpentinegalleries.org/files/downloads/181114_special-rights-wholebook.pdf.

someone, they will lose their sense of their own capability and self. Many children are pushed through a day that has little meaning for them at times, and we are missing the things that they can excel in because it doesn't fit with our perception of what they need. If a student has all-consuming anxiety, surely it would make sense to address that first to reduce their stress – and the teacher's – so an optimal learning state can be reached? Often, we bypass the fundamentals and it's like trying to build a house with no foundations. Trust in the relationship creates space for them to grow. Consistency and knowledge that tomorrow will build on today – or flexibly bend around a change in their health or well-being – can help them to feel at ease with their worries and to know that they can continue once they feel able to. If the world in which the student operates is different to yours, you need to join them in theirs to understand how you can help to create the pathway they need.

The key areas we have worked on have been relationships, trust, communication, connection, creativity, empathy and compassion. My daughter's future is now incredibly bright. I am still not sure what it will bring because we have the present to focus on, but it is now possible to think longer term and she is voicing or signing more and more around her preferences as she approaches adult-hood. What we would really like is for her to be able to fully express her own views on careers, and then we would work to find a way for her to pursue her goals.

Elly Chapple, disability campaigner

Company involvement through CSR: Anita Devi

Anita Devi is a specialist in supporting organisations to bring more diversity into the workforce, helping schools to support young people with SEND, and enabling more people with SEND to enter the workforce.[8]

---

8 See https://anitadevi.com/.

Case study: supporting young people with SEND in making career choices

Young people with SEND have dreams. They aspire to do things, see things, connect with others and be independent, just like everyone else. However, the way we go about supporting them may need to be different. In this piece, I will explore three vital and intentional actions that we can take to support young people with SEND: probe, listen, create, which we abbreviate to PLC. All names mentioned are pseudonyms, but their stories remain true and inspirational.

Probe

All learning begins with a question of sorts: something we want to find out. The same is true of young people with SEND. So, start by asking about their interests, what matters to them, what others think of them and, more importantly, how best to support them. A good way of approaching this is by using a person-centred tool, such as art therapy, and giving the young person the freedom to express their true thoughts, feelings, wishes and aspirations. Tools that don't rely on written words and can be created through audio or visual representation are helpful for some young people with SEND.

Having secured an initial response, it may be useful to probe a bit further. Sam's story demonstrates how this can make a difference.

Sam said he wanted to be an astronaut. He had thought a lot about this, and it was clear he wasn't just repeating something he had seen on television. Nor was he trying to please anyone. He was a bright young man, who had a lot of potential. However, whilst astronaut Tim Peake ran the London Marathon in space, we haven't quite developed the technology to take a wheelchair user and his carer into space. Sam was asked further questions around his purpose and goals. He did have a keen interest in all things astronomical but wasn't aware that desk-based jobs in several space agencies were also a possibility and that without these on-the-ground jobs astronauts can't function.

By asking the right questions, we can provide further information and open up new pathways for young people.

Listen

Listening is more than just hearing what is said; it is about understanding the person and their thinking. Sally's journey is a great example of this.

Sally struggled with reading, writing and anything academic. Her working memory was poor. She was way behind her peers. When asked what she wanted to do in terms of a career, Sally had only one answer: zookeeper. One teacher chose to listen and asked Sally two questions:

1. Have you ever visited the zoo?
2. What do you know about the animal feeding times?

In response to the first question, Sally said she had never been to the zoo! Although she struggled to read the time and information in general, she conveyed to her teacher how she would manage animal feeding times. Sally's career choice was not a whim, but something she had thought through in the context of her own learning difficulties. The teacher arranged for Sally to visit a zoo and meet the zookeeper. They clicked and the zookeeper kept in touch via online communications. This incentivised Sally in her studies. She didn't suddenly start getting top marks and she still struggles with reading, writing and numbers, but she feels she can be a zookeeper. All because someone took the time to listen.

More than printed information, meeting individuals who are doing the desired job is vital and gives young people a broader context of the role and how they could fit in, or not.

Create

We've all heard the cliché 'think outside the box'. Supporting young people with SEND is more than that; it's about not creating a box in the first place. It is easier to focus on what people can't do, but by focusing on 'abilities' – as opposed to 'disabilities' – opportunities emerge. These opportunities provide a structure and connectivity for young people with SEND. Imagine the opposite: a young person with SEND stuck at home, their only interaction is with carers and family and they have no purpose. Now imagine their thirtieth birthday, who would come to celebrate with them? A mother of a son on the autism spectrum recently shared one of her proudest moments: it was when her son stood next to his work colleagues during an apprenticeship and had his photo taken. He'd never had a peer group as a child. This young man now works for central government, undertaking repetitive tasks in finance. He enjoys his work and the government have a loyal, hard-working employee.

Alex couldn't read or write. She had no verbal communication either. A local company believed she had something to offer. They created a post with a badge that read 'data security officer'. Alex went in two days a week and shredded the firm's confidential papers. They trusted Alex and she enjoyed working with them, knowing that she could help and that what she did made a difference.

We can see what happens when we focus on what individuals bring to an organisation, not what they can't do.

Summary

Using the PLC model we have a structured system for supporting a young person with SEND into employment. As part of that structure, we need to consider the amount, quality and format of the information we provide. We need to consider how we build opportunities for practice in a safe space and, finally, how we can use concrete resources or technology to support the young person once they are in role, so they continue to make progress. For example, some companies use simulation software to teach tasks, others use videos. These are easily accessible, so the individual can go back and revisit as many times as they like. This is helpful after a period away from the workplace or when changes and challenges come up.

There is no easy one-size-fits-all solution, but the tenets of PLC provide a framework for engaging in dialogue and enabling young people with SEND in the workplace.

One final piece of advice – share the stories. Success breeds success. Sharing the success stories of young people with SEND inspires others to support them into the workplace.

Anita Devi, Founder and CEO #TeamADL CIC

Immersive vocational learning: Foxes Academy

Foxes Academy is a residential independent specialist college and training hotel for young adults with learning disabilities.[9] It's based in Minehead, Somerset, in the south-west of England. Hospitality training is delivered in a real, fully functioning working environment, Foxes Hotel, which is open to the public and has many outstanding reviews on TripAdvisor. Foxes Academy was the winner of the *TES* Overall FE Provider of the Year Award in 2018.[10] Between 2015 and 2018 an average of 8 out of 10 graduates from Foxes Academy (80%) got a job (in hospitality) compared to a national average of about 6% of people with a learning difficulty in paid employment.[11]

The Office for National Statistics 2019 disability and employment data showed that although the disability employment gap had reduced between 2013 and 2019, it is still significant: 53.2% of adults with a disability were in employment, whereas 81.8% adults without a disability were employed.[12]

The following case study from Clare Walsh at Foxes explains how they support the employability aspirations and skills of the young people who attend the academy.

---

9 See https://foxesacademy.ac.uk/.
10 Jonathan Owen, Winners of the TES FE Awards 2018 Announced, *TES* (24 February 2018). Available at: https://www.tes.com/news/winners-tes-fe-awards-2018-announced.
11 NHS Digital, Measures from the Adult Social Care Outcomes Framework, England 2017–18 (23 October 2018). Available at: https://digital.nhs.uk/data-and-information/publications/statistical/adult-social-care-outcomes-framework-ascof/current.
12 Office for National Statistics, Disability and Employment, UK: 2019 [statistical release] (2 December 2019). Available at: https://www.ons.gov.uk/peoplepopulationandcommunity/healthandsocialcare/disability/bulletins/disabilityandemploymentuk/2019#main-points.

Case study: careers at Foxes Academy

Foxes Academy has a huge impact on developing skills and attitudes for employability in people with SEND. Locally, Foxes has cultivated relationships with a number of employers and has a network of over 50 organisations that offer work experience placements, enabling students to transfer their skills and complete qualifications.

Teaching is geared to a key outcome from day one: employment. To support successful transition into work Foxes has cultivated formal partnerships with national employers in the hospitality and other sectors, including Hilton Hotels and the NHS. The hospitality sector was aiming to create more than 66,000 jobs and 200,000 new apprenticeships between 2018 and 2023.[13] The three-year course at Foxes Academy covers vocational qualifications and independent living skills, enabling the vast majority of students to gain long-term employment and the ability to move into independent accommodation.

The essential work-based qualifications recognised by employers are the NVQ Level 1 Certificate in Hospitality Services and the Level 1/2 Award in Food Safety. Students also study employability, transition and functional skills, and undertake work experience placements from Year 2 onwards.

In the year 2017–18 Foxes' students achieved 277 nationally recognised qualifications.[14] The curriculum and the range of support – such as speech and language therapy – are very effective, raising students' aspirations and enabling them to develop their independence and work skills.

One of the partnerships that has been created illustrates the importance of employers supporting young people in their career development. The Hilton Effect Foundation works with organisations worldwide that are making a positive impact on communities by providing funding and support. The Foundation has invested

---

13 UK Hospitality, *UK Hospitality Workforce Commission 2030 Report: The Changing Face of Hospitality* (September 2018), p. 5. Available at: https://www. youthemployment.org.uk/dev/wp-content/uploads/2018/09/UK-Hospitality-Workforce-Commission-2030.pdf.
14 Foxes Academy Prospectus. Available at: https://foxesacademy.ac.uk/wp-content/ uploads/2019/07/Foxes-Student-Brochure-05-06-19.pdf.

£40,000 in training facilities at Foxes Academy to further develop the skills of Foxes' students, with the long-term aim of making more work placements and jobs available to young people with SEND.

In 2016, after graduating from Foxes, Geor-Dan started working at Hilton Birmingham Metropole – the UK's largest conference hotel outside of London – as part of the larder kitchen team, preparing canapes and starters for guests at functions. Despite dealing with the daily challenges of ADHD and moderate learning difficulties, Geor-Dan has excelled in her role. She is a valued member of the team and has grown in confidence throughout her time at the hotel. She says:

I love the buzz of working in the kitchen at Hilton Birmingham Metropole. My training at Foxes and now my job have helped me to build my skills and become more confident. I've definitely learned a huge amount, including how to work quickly under pressure, which is really important when you work in a huge hotel! I love learning how to produce new dishes using the new set of knives I bought myself recently.

Geor-Dan's employer, chef Michael Lennon, says she has changed the atmosphere in the kitchen:

It's like a family as the team look out for Geor-Dan. She is reliable and always arrives early, then just gets on with the job. If I ever left I'd have to take her with me as she's so great in her role.

Clare Walsh, marketing manager, Foxes Academy

The three case studies in this chapter offer just a taste of the ways in which we can and must change our thinking and approach to delivering careers education to support students with SEND. Everybody has unique skills and qualities, and individuals and workplaces are missing out if their needs are not successfully and innovatively accommodated.

Supporting young people with SEND with their careers awareness and aspiration sometimes needs a bit more thought, but everyone deserves to envisage their own desired future and be offered the appropriate assistance to move towards it.

Chapter 9

BUSINESSES: THE HOW AND WHY OF INVOLVEMENT IN EDUCATION

People still need an ethical center, a sense of their role in society. A company can help fill that void if it shows its employees and customers that it understands its own ethical responsibilities and then can help them respond to their own.

Yvon Chouinard[1]

Know your region

Traditionally, different regions of the UK have had different specialisms and employment markets – Luton used to be the centre of hat making, Warrington was the great centre of wire, Lancashire was the home of cloth production, Sheffield steelworks, Stoke-on-Trent for pottery, Birkenhead, Newcastle and Glasgow were shipbuilding, etc. This regional variation occurs in countries around the world. Modern technology has made this notion less rigid than it once was for certain industries, but 'a place of work' is still the norm for most employees and so regional differences remain important when looking at career aspirations.

This chapter is certainly not about limiting your students' vision regarding their careers and should not be viewed as a constraint to their ambition; rather, it offers an acknowledgement that some of your students will want to stay local and others will want to move further afield to study, work and live. If a certain career ambition for a student is not fulfilled in the region, then this will be highlighted and a spotlight can be cast further afield.

Gatsby Benchmark 2 is rightly focused on learning from careers information and LMI. Although this isn't a guaranteed predictor of the

---

1   Yvon Chouinard, *Let My People Go Surfing: The Education of a Reluctant Businessman* (New York: Penguin, 2016), p. 230.

future of employment opportunities in a region, a knowledge of local, regional and national labour markets and the associated careers are good indicators of the possibilities.

At the time of writing, the regions of the UK have a number of LEPs and enterprise support functions set up to look after regional business development potential. They each support the key skills requirements of the region through initiatives including training, lobbying, partnerships between employers and educators (schools, colleges, apprenticeship providers and universities), networking and, in some cases, regional development funding. LEPs also work with government vehicles including the National Careers Service and the Careers and Enterprise Company to provide local LMI and deliver support to schools within the region. They are now rolling out a number of regional Careers Hubs to support more focused development in areas of high need (i.e. the cold spots identified in Chapter 3).[2]

The LEPs and Careers Hubs will have their fingers on the pulse with regard to insights about local companies and industries and their future skills requirements. In addition to fact-finding and support for your students, use this local knowledge to inform the five- or ten-year plans for your subject specialisms and qualifications – this is the true value of local LMI. (The Foxes Academy partnership with the Hilton Effect Foundation in Chapter 8 shows the importance of creating relationships with businesses to equip young people with in-demand skills.)

Similarly, local universities and FE colleges, Chambers of Commerce, Rotary clubs, Business in the Community and professional bodies should be able to help your students to look ahead and develop their skills by providing research, predictions, employer talks and assemblies, and a range of work experience opportunities.

Many schools and colleges will develop strong links to local businesses – especially local businesses that are part of a larger enterprise – and these links will have multiple benefits for the educational institution, so should be encouraged and nurtured. Benefits that businesses can bring to schools include:

- Providing insight through assemblies and interview skills days.
- Helping with work experience and maybe future internship offers.

2 See https://www.careersandenterprise.co.uk/about-us/our-network/careers-hubs.

- Enabling staff – and possibly students – to attend networking events. Opportunities to host business network events at the school premises will extend the partnership.

- Collaborative learning opportunities for students – possibly offering joint qualifications or apprenticeships to meet the future skills needs of the businesses.

These benefits can be accrued by getting in touch with local businesses and business networks to see who would like to work with you and your students. This chapter gives more advice about how to attract local businesses to support your school and Chapter 10 suggests a number of questions to help any teacher (or possibly student) approach outside organisations for support. We also saw in Chapter 4 how engaging parents by setting up a PCA can help. Not only would a PCA encourage parental engagement, but parents – through their local contacts and links – could also help to leverage local businesses' knowledge and experience into the school.

Local chapters of the CBI, Careers Hubs linked to local Chambers of Commerce and regional development plans (for example, the Northern Powerhouse initiative[3]) will all have an impact on long-term planning for employability, training, learning and school engagement. One region of the UK which is benefitting from strong links between local employers, educational establishments and a longer-term regional vision is the Humber, with the city of Hull at its heart: the development of the Energy Estuary provides a vision for investment in infrastructure and people. (See details and links under the WiME project in Chapter 6.)

The careers lead in your school should initiate investigations into regional developments and longer-term plans; however, *every* teacher can benefit from the additional context that local links will bring to the classroom.

---

3   See https://northernpowerhouse.gov.uk/.

Research tasks to set for students

It's great if teachers point students to a website or give them a hand-out, isn't it? However, we learn more when we are set a task. It also helps to increase capabilities around the 7SAS, especially accessing and analysing information, critical thinking and problem solving and – if students have to present or write up their findings – effective oral and written communication.

Here are a number of simple questions to set during form time, for homework or in preparation for work experience, options decisions or mock interviews.

What are the skills needs in our local area? (Or another area/region/city.)

What skills might local employers need now and in the future?

What investment plans are there for our region? Is this different from other regions?

Which employers work with local universities and colleges to meet these skills needs?

Which local educational institutions support the pathways into – for example – nursing, electrical engineering, sports psychology, music technology, web design and IT, equine studies, dentistry, primary teaching, etc.?

What are the traditional skills of our region? How have these changed in the past century and how are they likely to change in the next two decades?

Where in the country is the highest demand for: construction workers, language therapists, translators, architects, civil engineers, digital skills, marine technologists, automotive designers, chefs, etc.?

Where are the biggest growth areas in – for example – technology, creative work, automation, healthcare, teaching, sports, etc. in the next decade and how do these compare with our region?

It is definitely worth pointing students to research completed by the Careers and Enterprise Company on the nation's cold spots, where careers learning is lacking and traditional industries have been phased out and not replaced, leading to a dearth of available jobs. The Edge Foundation is an education charity that performs research and interventions in local areas to increase opportunity and equality in education. As they say on their website:

We believe a coherent, unified and holistic education system can support social equity and enable all young people to fulfil their potential.[4]

The Edge Foundation also researches skills shortages, launching a report in 2019 which suggested that localism is 'key to addressing skill shortage crisis'.[5] This highlights that there are agencies in the UK that are working together to reduce skills gaps and focus on the development of local solutions. Because this research applies to many regions of the UK the focus should not just be limited to your region but could be spread more widely.

A side benefit of tasking students to do this research is that they will get to see comparisons between regions and hopefully gain a better understanding of the concept and reality of moving away and the possibilities that will open up in different regions of the country, continent and world.

Ask them to present their findings as infographics or posters, which could be used in corridors or the careers, or conventional, library. Then spend some time debating the benefits and opportunities of developing certain skills in region X or Y. Looking at multiple sources of data and research will be helpful:

- Office for National Statistics will give national and regional trends in employment, industry and employability.[6]

- National Careers Service lists over 800 job descriptions and profiles.[7]

- LEPs will help with local initiatives based on regional skills needs.

- LEP Growth Hubs are based on research on skills needs and can be a resource for discovering regional skills needs.[8]

---

4 See https://www.edge.co.uk/about-us.
5 The Edge Foundation, Localism Key to Addressing Skill Shortage Crisis, Says Edge Foundation (12 November 2019). Available at: https://www.edge.co.uk/news/edge-news/skills-shortages-bulletin-6.
6 See https://www.ons.gov.uk/employmentandlabourmarket.
7 See https://nationalcareers.service.gov.uk/.
8 See https://www.lepnetwork.net.

- Contacting local FE colleges and universities will be instructive in seeing which courses are available to satisfy local and regional skills and knowledge needs.

Researching local skills gaps and employability is likely not very inherently exciting for your students, but by understanding the local labour market and what is needed, available, growing or shrinking within local industries in different regions of the country (and what skills will be needed in the next 10 or more years) students will hopefully appreciate the valuable insight into how *they* themselves will fit into the future.

Context is everything: for some students, the local context will be a vital part of their decision-making in their choice of options, subjects and activities and will raise awareness of, and aspirations in, particular directions – whether local or not. Some students may have already set their sights elsewhere.

The acquisition of local and regional knowledge can – for the teacher, SLT member or governor interested in careers and enterprise learning – be instructional in developing the curriculum and relationships with FE and HE providers and local employers. When you know what the local and regional economy needs and what the necessary steps are to get your young people ready to satisfy that need, your requests for support are more accurate and powerful. Local knowledge, therefore, can support the development of partnerships which can and should encourage businesses to send the career ladder down to young people to give them a step up. These relationships can support Gatsby Benchmarks 2 and 4, with meaningful links made to 3, 5, 6, 7 and 8 when local knowledge is acted upon.

When schools understand their local and regional skills needs, and combine this knowledge with appropriate personal guidance, ambitions and pathways can then be explored with each young person individually. This one-to-one guidance must be used to explore training, study and career options across every subject and location to ensure students don't feel as if they are being corralled onto a conveyor belt of predictable outcomes.

Tick-box interviews help no one.

How to get local businesses and organisations involved in supporting your students

Self-reflection task

Have a think back to all the times you were given a chance to experience or understand a workplace or industry – perhaps through a work experience placement, visit, hobby, lesson, film, TV programme or discussion.

Reflect on this and on whether any of these experiences changed the course of your life. What could you do to build relationships with local organisations so they can help to offer some of these experiences to the young people in your area?

In Chapter 1 we saw how 36% of employers surveyed thought that 16-year-olds were 'poorly or very poorly' prepared for work, whilst 29% said the same about 17–18-year-olds.[9] If businesses can't find appropriately skilled or work-ready school-leavers then surely it should be at least partially incumbent on those businesses to support schools and colleges to ready young people for work?

I've spoken to many business leaders who say they've tried to speak to their local school only to be ignored or to have their calls go unreturned. In some cases, businesses have spoken to someone at the school who doesn't know what they can gain from a business relationship. This chapter will help you to forge and get the best out of these relationships, in order to strengthen the mutual support network for our young people.

If activity between businesses and schools is part of a structured programme of development, we can reasonably assume that the strategies discussed here will help your school, academy or educational establishment to meet Gatsby Benchmark 1. I will also detail how the remaining Gatsby Benchmarks link to these strategies.

9   Careers and Enterprise Company, *Prioritisation Index 2015*, p. 13.

Businesses local to you might be struggling to find the right staff, so wouldn't it be positive if working in partnership would help your students with real-world careers advice, work experience and understanding with a possible longer-term side benefit of some of your students to find appropriate opportunities locally?

Making contact

Work out exactly what you need

All schools will need something different: some will have solid plans for careers engagement through the different years, some will have a strategy to follow, some will have a careers lead and SLT plan for industry and business engagement. What is your school's plan? Is it subject-specific? Once you have knowledge of your school's plan, you will be able to see if anything is missing and if your knowledge, skills and connections can be brought into action.

There will be a number of assets in any local business or organisation that will be valued and required by your school (and I don't just mean funding to help buy new PE kit, an espresso machine or some wood-chip for the new well-being garden). For example:

- An assembly talk from a local business owner with an interesting life or career story.
- Professionals or tradespeople giving inspiring demonstrations to your students during lessons.
- Local sports clubs delivering PE sessions.
- Local farmers discussing their processes in food technology.
- Local bands/musicians/actors working with your music or drama department.

Make sure that in any communication with local businesses you reassure them that red tape and DBS checks aren't likely to be an issue – in most cases these won't be needed because visitors will be chaperoned by members of staff and won't be left alone with students. If DBS checks are needed, offer help to facilitate checks for any company staff involved in supporting the school over a longer time period.

Contact the right person to ask for help

It's important to understand that a business receptionist's job – as in schools – is to be concerned with the staff's time management, so they don't want just anyone calling up to 'have a chat'. Their time is finite and pressured. Clearly, you need to be specific in your request – or list of needs – so whoever answers the phone or forwards the email can put you through to the right person. This is not to denigrate any requests you may have, more to help you understand that you may have to try a number of times to find the right contact. Being succinct will help.

Call and ask to speak to one of the following with your request for help or support:

- The managing director.
- The human resources (HR) manager in charge of careers and employability.
- The director in charge of recruitment and apprenticeships.
- The CSR (or social responsibility or community) manager.
- The head of marketing or communications.

You may have to send an email or letter to outline your request. Don't give up after the first try – companies have different policies and procedures. You could even try to visit organisations at lunchtime or at the end of the day to drop information off for the appropriate team member.

Invite them in to the school

Once you've made contact with the appropriate person at the business, arrange for them to visit the school premises to have a look around and discuss how they could help you. It is worth pointing out that until they know what you want, they may not think they have anything to offer your school.

Sometimes you will know exactly what your school needs from them – for example, support for your IT department's digital design projects or someone to talk to students about the role of a solicitor, or what a project manager does or how MFL is used in careers. Sometimes you may not know exactly what the local business can offer, so the conversation at this point is really important in terms of establishing what the business could do to help. Like any relationship, it takes time and we don't know what we don't know. The process of talking about possibilities is exciting and can bring forward ideas that have not even been considered. You could also ask your friends and family if their employers could help.

Asking for help

The following ideas may or may not be possible or practical in your school but hopefully this list will act as inspiration.

Ask if the business can offer work experience placements

These are usually week-long placements for Year 10 students to give them an overview of the business and industry. It's important that students are given a variety of insights into the world of work, so it would be beneficial if they could shadow various individuals across different roles in the company. Some businesses also offer leadership placements in which students work alongside members of the board of directors.

Gatsby Benchmarks: 1, 2, 3, 4, 5, 6 and 8.

Real-world projects

Suggest that the business commissions projects for your students to undertake – for example, a website review or analysis of how the organisation could use social media to encourage engagement. This could be part of work experience or a stand-alone project set up around a specific subject area. For example: design a new logo (art); translate web pages or leaflets into French, German or Cantonese (MFL); write, edit or proofread web pages or documents (English); develop social media profiles to support marketing (art, IT and English).

Gatsby Benchmarks: 1, 3, 4, 5 and 6.

Annual project competition

Could the organisation work with you to design a curriculum-linked project or competition/challenge for students? Students could submit entries for the business to choose a winner. These projects should be tangible and realistic – perhaps a restaurant could ask local schools to design a new dish; a design company could ask for ideas for a new building; companies in any industry could ask students to come up with a campaign to attract young people to work at their business.

The beauty of these ideas is that the submissions will provide powerful ideas for business development and better engagement with young people. Another benefit is that the submissions – whether posters, digital or reports – can be displayed in the school and/or the business to advertise the partnership. Once these challenges are established they will be easier to administer and repeat. (These ideas form the backbone of the Dream Placement and Make It schemes explored in Chapter 7.)

Gatsby Benchmarks: 1, 3, 4, 5 and 6.

Challenge the business to do something really brave

They could task a team of young people to give the company a report on how they could be more environmentally friendly, ask a team of geography students to advise on how to increase the number of employees walking or cycling to work, trust a young person to take over their corporate Twitter or Instagram account for the day, ask a team of young people to perform a dance or drama piece in the canteen at lunchtime, or challenge students to rebrand the business or to look at the organisation's processes and see if they can make the company more efficient.

Gatsby Benchmarks: 1, 2, 3, 4, 5, 6 and 8.

Ask staff members to mentor students

This is especially important for students who are interested in breaking into industries in which they are under-represented. If an organisation is looking to attract more women or people from BAME backgrounds into leadership, for example, then visibility is key to allowing young people to believe that *they* could pursue that career.

Mentoring could be the difference between a student taking their GCSEs seriously or not. Mentors do not need to be senior members of staff. In fact, apprentices might be of a similar age and background to the students, so they could be ideally placed to bridge the gap between what students think is 'not for them' and their skills and abilities.

Mentoring could involve regular one-to-one or group sessions in which the mentor would support students in their day-to-day learning and motivation whilst at the same time inspiring them towards a bigger long-term goal. This has advantages for the staff members too as they will be developing valuable confidence, influence, leadership skills and potentially qualifications.

Gatsby Benchmarks: 1, 2, 3, 4, 5 and 8.

Ask staff to volunteer locally with students

They could do litter picks, sports coaching, or start clubs to support student and volunteering interest in different sports and hobbies. (Clearly safeguarding and chaperoning guidelines are important here and should be carefully considered for each event you plan.)

Gatsby Benchmarks: 1, 3, 4, 5, 6 and 8.

Ask the company to deliver an assembly

They could give a presentation about their business and industry, including the careers opportunities available. It's important to stress that the company shouldn't assume the students know anything about their organisation, even if it's on the doorstep of the school.

Gatsby Benchmarks: 1, 2, 4, 5 and 6.

Ask them to help with interview skills

Interview skills days typically involve company representatives volunteering to mock interview young people for their ideal job. This is a crucial confidence-building activity for students and will help prepare them for the next phase of life. The staff involved get the benefit of connecting with young people and perhaps updating their view of teenagers! Linking these experiences with pathway discussions about FE and HE also provides powerful inspiration.

Gatsby Benchmarks: 1, 2, 3, 4, 5, 6, 7 and 8.

Ask them to help during a national awareness week

Examples could include: Engineering Week, Arts Week, NCW, Anti-Bullying Week, Global Entrepreneurship Week, Macmillan coffee mornings, etc. These awareness events or weeks are often supported in schools as well as businesses and may give companies the chance to deliver an assembly or similar. In addition, if a business always 'wants to get involved' but somehow never finds the time, then using this opportunity could be just the *excuse* the organisation needs to support others and carry out some CSR or social enterprise locally.

Gatsby Benchmarks: 1, 2, 4, 5 and 6.

Offer to run a business event at the school

A networking event or conference could use the school's facilities, with students working behind the scenes with company staff to control IT, parking, ticketing, etc. In this way students get real-life work experience and the ability to work alongside businesspeople from the organisation. Examples could include a morning networking event, an early evening product launch or a whole-day conference which could be held during the holidays when school is closed.

I was invited to an event like this at a school in Southport by a friend and network partner who is the head teacher. The school invited businesses to come into the school with a view to creating a business support network. The event had a number of purposes: businesses linking locally; discussion of the school's needs; business leaders meeting subject leaders; and discussing skills needs for the future and ideas for school–business partnerships. There was even talk of allowing young people to be ambassadors for the school and to help plan and project-manage similar events.

Gatsby Benchmarks: 1, 2, 3, 4, 5, 6 and 8.

Networking

Ask if the local business is part of a local business or charity network – perhaps the local Chamber of Commerce, Rotary club or business networking organisation. You need to see if there is any appetite for support amongst your local business and community networks. Do students, parents, governors or staff have any contacts in the business community?

Gatsby Benchmarks: 2, 3, 4, 5, 6 and 8.

Think of other project ideas

What could inspire, support and encourage the local business community to help young people in your school? Take this chapter as inspiration and think of your own ways of linking with businesses to develop a meaningful project. If you need help, get on Twitter and speak to careers experts who could support you with ideas for engagement – especially search for #NCW2020 and #NCW2021 (or substitute the year in which you are reading this) for ideas and examples. Projects could include award ceremony sponsorships, company visits, factory tours, focus panels, discussion groups, sports events or fun days sponsored by local businesses.

Conclusion

As ever, these are ideas, examples and proposals – you, your school and local organisations may do things differently. If you do and are proud of the results of your endeavours, please take to Twitter and share them using #SetUpTheLadder or tagging me @EnterpriseSBox.

Finally, the more radical and innovative ideas could secure you a few column inches in the local paper, and all successful collaborations could be mentioned in the school's social media and the PR for the supporting business or organisations involved. These promotional opportunities should, of course, be seen as a side benefit of supporting young people. Supporting the next generation is its own reward – but being able to evidence CSR might entice more businesses and organisations to get involved.

Try it.

Chapter 10
CAREERS QUESTIONS

The important thing is not to stop questioning. Curiosity has its own reason for existing.

Albert Einstein[1]

Questioning is a valuable tool which can help us to support young people in terms of thinking about the career they want, the skills they might need and the pathway they might take. Questions are also valuable for the school in terms of reflecting on the careers education on offer.

As such, this chapter lists questions which will be helpful in a variety of situations. They are grouped together in terms of their purpose and who will be doing the asking. It's worth deciding between the SLT and careers leads who is going to speak to whom. I have heard many anecdotal examples of different teachers and leaders all asking the same external organisations for the same thing, which causes confusion and frustration.

Internally, school staff – especially reception staff – need to know how to route and refer any calls which come through of an external careers support nature so that these leads and possibilities aren't lost. If someone from a business calls your school for the first time and is misdirected or misunderstood, they may not call again.

---

1 Albert Einstein, statement to William Miller, quoted in *LIFE* magazine (2 May 1955). For discussion of the source, see: https://quoteinvestigator.com/2017/11/20/value/.

Questions for teachers to ask of themselves and their colleagues, then discuss with students

Who helped me in my career?

Why did I make the choices I made?

Did I make any 'wrong' decisions?

Did I listen to any advice? From whom? About what?

What was my first job?

What did I think I would end up doing?

What was my ideal career aged 8, 15, 20, 26, etc.?

What was my *dream* job?

Regarding the careers context Venn diagram in Chapter 1, in percentage terms how important is each element (peers, parents, education and employers)? How has each affected me?

Am I happy?

What does 'happy' mean to me?

Is the career horizon for young people harder to navigate than it was for me and my peers?

What was my worst/best interview?

Was my career journey harder or easier than my parents' was? Why is that?

What would I tell my 16-year-old self?

What would improve my quality of life?

What would I not want to regret in the future in relation to my career?

How does/could my subject area link learning to careers?

How could we meet more of the Gatsby Benchmarks?

What is the best way to support careers learning in my subject?

Is careers learning *really* structured and well-managed in our school?

How could we make our careers provision better for every student?

Questions for teachers to ask of primary students

What do you love doing?

Where do people work?

How do you help people?

How do you solve problems?

Who do you ask for help when you need it?

Are you good at making decisions?

Can you make a list of 20 different jobs? (If you need ideas, think about your family, neighbours, people you meet on journeys and people who help us.)

What would be the most exciting job in the world ever?

What job would be the most helpful to others?

Which jobs use maths the most?

What is the smelliest job in the world?

Which job makes people the happiest?

What do you love to learn about the most?

Are there any jobs that would be scary? Why?

Are there any jobs that would be really fun? Why?

What is your *dream* job?

What job would make someone important?

Questions for teachers to ask of secondary (and above) students

Which of your subjects do you think will be most useful for your career?

Where do you see yourself in 5, 10, 15, 20 years?

How can your skills help others?

What do you love to do?

Can you make a list of 30, 40 or 50 different jobs?

(Using the 7SAS) How do you display each of your seven skills now?

Where do your talents lie?

Where are you at your happiest and why?

When are you happiest? (The CASK Wheel of Life can help here.)

How do you know if someone has lived a worthwhile life?

What makes life worth living?

How do you measure success?

How do you know if you're a successful person?

What are the *true* measures of success?

When do you expect to stop learning?

What is your greatest achievement?

Which skills have you developed outside of school or formal education?

Could these skills lead to a career? How?

Which school subjects do you think relate best to the career you want for yourself?

If you could not fail, what would you choose to do?

What job would you *not* want to do?

Which jobs will disappear in the next 20 years? Why? What about the next 120 years?

Which jobs will be replaced by AI or robots in the future?

What is the best source of information about careers?

Who do you trust to advise you about careers?

Which jobs have been created in the past 10 years?

If you could do any one thing for the rest of your life, what would it be? Would you want to do the same thing forever?

What is happiness in a career?

When do you want to retire from work?

Is having a purpose essential for you to enjoy your life?

How long do you think your main job will last?

How many jobs or careers do you think you'll undertake in total before you retire?

Have you made any mistakes so far?

What have you learned about yourself from making mistakes?

Look at the STAR Model (from the CASK). When have you been a star recently? Give me two examples.

What are your best habits and behaviours?

What do you want to improve about yourself? And *how* will you do this?

What are you most proud of yourself for?

What does your *ideal* future look like?

What is your next step?

How could you prepare yourself for your future?

Questions for careers leads, teachers and governors to ask of businesses

How could your organisation support our school?

How was your careers education? Can you help make our students' experience better than yours was?

We are trying to meet the eight Gatsby Benchmarks – would you help us? What support might you be able to offer?

Could your organisation donate some of your CSR time or funds to help our students?

Do you run any initiatives to promote your business and industry in the local community?

What skills do your staff have that could support our SLT?

Who helped you in your career?

What are the key skills your industry is looking for in the next five to ten years?

Does your company struggle to find people with the right skills? (If so, what are the skills you most want to see in recruits?)

Do you expect young people to be work-ready? If so, how should this happen?

How do you support your staff's career development?

Is there anyone in your organisation who would like to come and speak to students in an assembly?

Do you have any young staff members/apprentices who could come and speak to our students?

Could any of your team come and help with mock interviews?

Could you help with developing skills for the future – part-time work, making a good impression, etc.?

Do you have any team building exercises we could use with our students?

Could we – either a teacher or some students – come and visit your workplace?

Would your organisation consider supporting the funding of our online careers package for students?

Would your organisation design a challenge which could engage our students and help them gain an understanding of your business and industry?

Do you have a real-world project which could be used as a challenge for our students in some way?

How could you help our students to understand your industry?

How could you help our students learn about running their own businesses?

Do you ever sponsor or fund careers-related activities?

Do you get involved with any charity events? Could our school get involved too?

Questions for careers leads to ask of the SLT

How will we support our teaching staff to implement the Gatsby Benchmarks?

What is my time allowance for CEIAG activities?

What is my budget?

Can we afford *not* to support CEIAG?

How do we best prepare our young people for the rest of their lives?

Who will be my day-to-day contact on the SLT?

How will we measure our CEIAG provision effectively?

What are the guidelines for contacting local businesses and employers?

Do I have agreement to get involved in regional and national initiatives and competitions as I see fit?

Can we ask suppliers and contractors who tender with us to add CSR to their contract and deliver some work experience, talks or challenges for our students?

How can we encourage a sense of pride in achievements?

Can we start a careers club in Key Stage 3?

What support/funding is available for an online careers toolkit (e.g. Compass+[2])?

Could we add a standard agenda item on careers to full governor meetings?

Could I present a careers update to the governors at every full meeting?

Can we set up a PCA alongside the PTA?

Can we put NCW/Apprenticeship Week/Global Entrepreneurship Week/Science Week into our school calendar and plan events accordingly?[3]

Questions for careers leads to ask of colleagues

Remember that subject teachers already have a lot on their plates; these suggestions are meant as simple prompts to increase the depth and relevance of their subject in terms of students thinking about their futures.

Are there any areas of your subject which could be brought to life by an outside speaker or business connection?

How can I help you to connect with more outside influences to support your subject?

How could you bring more careers and enterprise thinking into your subject area?

Did you have any different jobs before becoming a teacher which could inspire and inform your classes?

---

2   See https://www.careersandenterprise.co.uk/schools-colleges/compass-plus.
3   For free resources, see: https://nationalcareersweek.com/.

If we have an event for NCW in school, what could you help with?

Do you have any friends, family members or connections who would be willing to talk about their job in an assembly or similar?

Which of the CASK tools are you using?

How could you use any of the subject stepladders (Chapter 5) in your subject?

Who inspired you earlier in life?

OK, these are just your starters for 10. I know there will be hundreds more good questions you could ask and I'm sure you will. Use #SetUpTheLadder to share your questions and, importantly, the results you achieve.

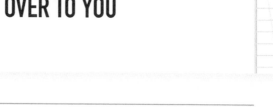

Chapter 11

OVER TO YOU

I stand by the fact that I am a yes person. In every job I have had, I put my hand up to volunteer for the thing that scares me.

Jess Phillips MP[1]

Marginal gains is the concept of making small adjustments – for example, to process, design, application and development – which, when added together, make positive results more likely. Marginal gains has been cited as instrumental in the renaissance and success of British Cycling in the first part of the 21st century.

Former Olympic champion and head of the 'Secret Squirrel Club' at British Cycling Chris Boardman says:

In the run-up to the Beijing Olympics we gained a huge under-standing. We didn't just try to make a big improvement in one area; we looked at a thousand things, and how each could be improved by just one per cent. Aggregate all of that and it becomes a meaning-ful number.[2]

Marginal gains is a concept which I hope you will see mirrored in this book, in the CASK and in the idea that, alongside academic learning, if we make small adjustments to the concept of personal development and career awareness using a simple set of tools, then young people will gain exponentially.

As I said at the start of this book, teachers are busy people and don't need any more 'initiatives' to implement. However, when it comes to the overall education and development of the young people in our charge, I believe that we are all responsible for making their journey

---

1   Jess Phillips, *Everywoman: One Woman's Truth about Speaking the Truth* (London: Hutchinson, 2017), p. 39.
2   Chris Boardman, My Nine Years with British Cycling, *BBC Sport* (6 April 2012). Available at: https://www.bbc.co.uk/sport/cycling/17635921.

through school and into adulthood more fulfilling and informed. It's not just the pursuit of money via a career that drives this book and the concepts within it; education needs to focus on well-being, personal fulfilment and a sense of purpose.

PSHEE is crucial if young people are to develop a considered world view, as well as broader ideas and horizons. Part of the aim of CEIAG *has* to be students gaining the belief to say to themselves, 'Wow, I could do *anything* in my future!' Sometimes parents aren't able to offer the space, mindset, well-being and time to help their children question the possibilities, but I believe that every child deserves to have that chance. Schools must find the time to ask these questions with them.

Do not underestimate the role of informed confidence in a young person. Someone who has reflected regularly on their learning and skills, and can plot their personal development, will be much better able to express themselves on paper and in person. These skills work to support academic and practical progress and act as a bridge to realising career ambitions as young people transition from school towards employment, whichever route they take. Hence why the CASK is so useful.

Transitions are a key stage in our lives: childhood to adolescence, learner to employee, trainee to trainer. They offer opportunities for lost confidence or growth of ability. The CASK offers scaffolding which helps to build self-confidence through self-awareness and familiarity. By knowing who we are and becoming aware of our skills and abilities, we are better able to negotiate new and potentially challenging experiences with more self-belief and a sense of control.

This book and the ideas, tools, resources and reasons behind it are my attempt to make personal development and deeper careers and enterprise learning an incremental and possible objective. I hope this book shows that it doesn't require a fundamental change in practice to develop career and self-awareness alongside academic learning. By using slightly different thinking, a structured approach and simple tools, we can enable our young people to continually review their skills, behaviours and attitudes. At the centre of the CASK is a celebration of every individual.

What is more, individuals need to be equipped to cope with change. Across the globe political and economic uncertainty is increasing. The world of work is changing in many ways, with contract changes, industrial developments, the move to more sustainable technologies and different working patterns. New products are being invented every day and new systems created. Schools and educational establishments are under increasing pressure to deliver new skills, new qualifications and keep up with changes in educational policy and outcomes, as well as responding to the needs of learners and the wider world.

For most young people, pursuing a university education will mean accruing a considerable debt. Young people are less likely to be able to afford a house than in previous generations and the generational gulf is growing year on year. Social mobility is stagnating despite advances in affordable technology (we saw the details on inequality and research into social mobility in Chapter 3). More than ever before, young people in the UK and across the world are competing for jobs with less security and lower pay.

So?

This book is based on my belief that we have a duty, once we have climbed a step (or two, or three) on the career ladder and are in a stable position ourselves, to send the ladder back down to support young people who are starting out in the world of work.

I'm convinced that where possible we need to provide young people with:

- Help with career awareness.
- Help with work experience.
- Help with self-reflection and skills awareness.
- Help with making connections.
- Help with mentoring.
- Help with paid internships.
- Help with self-employment.
- Help with entrepreneurship.
- Help with whatever it is that they need to allow them to enjoy a career that suits them, pays them fairly and is fulfilling and purposeful.

I want you to ask yourself:

Who helped me?

What can I do to help someone else?

Who can I help?

How can I help them?

What can I do *today*?

Thank you.

Bernie

APPENDIX: GETTING INVOLVED

You can find me on Twitter: @EnterpriseSBox.

Or on my company website: https://innovativeenterprise.co.uk.

Clearly there is also Instagram, Facebook and a host of other social media platforms, as well as various careers forums and systems that your organisation might use.

I'm keen that you use the ideas in this book, deploy them, apply them, improve them, discuss them and share them with colleagues in education and business across the UK. Please do not hesitate to suggest improvements – connect through Twitter or contact me though the website link. Send me your hints and tips and I'll share them for others to use and benefit from.

If you do share your ideas, please use #SetUpTheLadder.

Whatever you do, please start and continue to support young people with their career thinking, options and decisions, and encourage others in business, industry, charity and across education to do the same. I'd be delighted if everyone who reads this book would share and recommend it and become part of a movement that will, alongside teaching and education, change young people's lives for the better in the long term.

REFERENCES

Attwood, Rebecca (2009). 'Not for the Likes of Us', *Times Higher Education* (12 August). Available at: https://timeshighereducation.com/news/not-for-the-likes-of-us/407750.article.

BAE Systems (2019). *Future Skills for Our UK Business: A Whitepaper* (June). Available at: https://www.baesystems.com/en/our-company/skills-and-education/future-skills-for-our-uk-business.

Barnes, Sally-Anne, Jenny Bimrose, Alan Brown, John Gough and Sally Wright (2020). *The Role of Parents and Carers in Providing Careers Guidance and How They Could Be Better Supported* (Warwick: University of Warwick). Available at: https://warwick.ac.uk/fac/soc/ier/research/careerguidanceparents/ier_gatsby_jpm_parents-carers_final_report_v8_final.pdf.

BBC News (2019). Creative Subjects: The £100bn Industry 'Neglected by Schools' (5 September). Available at: https://www.bbc.co.uk/news/av/uk-england-london-49579764/creative-subjects-the-100bn-industry-neglected-by-schools.

Bennett, Rosemary (2019). Case Study: 'The Minute I Heard About the BTec I Was Instantly Excited', *The Times* (24 August). Available at: https://thetimes.co.uk/article/case-study-the-minute-i-heard-about-the-btec-i-was-instantly-excited-plk8nqgzn.

Bernard, Andrew (2016). 'Engineering Random Opportunities to Succeed', *TEDxWhitehaven* (14 October). Available at: https://youtu.be/BILhkke2sfQ.

BMG Research (2013). *New GCSE Grades Research Amongst Employers* [research report prepared for Ofqual] (November). Available at: https://assets.publishing.service.gov.uk/government/uploads/system/uploads/attachment_data/file/529390/2013-11-01-bmg-research-with-employers-on-new-gcse-grades.pdf.

Boardman, Chris (2012). My Nine Years with British Cycling, *BBC Sport* (6 April). Available at: https://www.bbc.co.uk/sport/cycling/17635921.

British Chambers of Commerce (2015). BCC: Businesses and schools 'still worlds apart' on readiness for work [press release] (11 November). Available at: https://www.britishchambers.org.uk/news/2015/11/bcc-businesses-and-schools-still-worlds-apart-on-readiness-for-work.

Careers and Enterprise Company (2015). *Prioritisation Index 2015: Cold Spots*. Available at: https://www.careersandenterprise.co.uk/sites/default/files/uploaded/cold_spots_report_2015.pdf.

Careers and Enterprise Company (2018). *Updating the Careers Cold Spots: The Careers and Enterprise Prioritisation Indicators*. Available at: https://www.careersandenterprise.co.uk/sites/default/files/uploaded/updating_the_careers_cold_spots_report.pdf.

Careers and Enterprise Company (2019). *State of the Nation 2019: Progress Towards the Gatsby Benchmarks in England's Secondary Schools and Colleges in Local Enterprise Partnerships.* Available at: https://www.careersandenterprise.co.uk/sites/default/files/uploaded/1273_state_of_the_nation_lep_analysis_2019_final_1019.pdf.

Careers and Enterprise Company (2020). Workplace skills now more important than exam results in post-Covid jobs market say teachers (7 July). Available at: https://www.careersandenterprise.co.uk/news/workplace-skills-now-more-important-exam-results-post-covid-jobs-market-say-teachers.

Carr, Flora (2017). The New GCSE Grades: An Employer's Perspective, *Daily Telegraph* (23 August). Available at: https://www.telegraph.co.uk/education/0/new-gcse-grades-employers-perspective/.

Chambers, Nick, Elnaz T. Kashefpakdel, Jordan Rehill and Christian Percy (2018). *Drawing the Future: Exploring the Career Aspirations of Primary School Children from Around the World* (London: Education and Employers). Available at: https://www.educationandemployers.org/wp-content/uploads/2018/01/Drawing-the-Future-FINAL-REPORT.pdf.

Chartered Management Institute (2019). Apprenticeships Make the Grade [press release] (14 August). Available at: https://www.managers.org.uk/about-us/media-centre/cmi-press-releases/apprenticeships-make-the-grade.

Chouinard, Yvon (2016). *Let My People Go Surfing: The Education of a Reluctant Businessman* (New York: Penguin).

Coughlan, Sean (2019). Careers Ambitions 'Already Limited by Age of Seven', *BBC News* (15 October). Available at: https://www.bbc.co.uk/news/amp/education-50042459.

Davies, Howard (2002). *Review of Enterprise and the Economy in Education* (February). Available at: https://www.readyunlimited.com/wp-content/uploads/2011/09/Davies-Review-main-doc.pdf.

de Vries, Robert and Jason Rentfrow (2016). *A Winning Personality: The Effects of Background on Personality and Earnings* (London: The Sutton Trust). Available at: https://www.suttontrust.com/research-paper/a-winning-personality-confidence-aspirations-social-mobility/.

Department for Business, Energy and Industrial Strategy (2020). Business Population Estimates for the UK and Regions: 2019 Statistical Release (14 January). Available at: https://www.gov.uk/government/publications/business-population-estimates-2019/business-population-estimates-for-the-uk-and-regions-2019-statistical-release-html.

Department for Education (2017). *Careers Strategy: Making the Most of Everyone's Skills and Talents.* Ref: DFE-00310-2017 (December). Available at: https://assets.publishing.service.gov.uk/government/uploads/system/uploads/attachment_data/file/664319/Careers_strategy.pdf.

Department for Education (2018). *Careers Guidance and Access for Education and Training Providers: Statutory Guidance for Governing Bodies, School Leaders and School Staff.* Ref: DFE-00002-2018 (October). Available at: https://assets.publishing.service.gov.uk/government/uploads/system/uploads/attachment_data/file/748474/181008_schools_statutory_guidance_final.pdf.

Department for Education (2019). Schools, Pupils and Their Characteristics [statistical release] (January). Available at: https://assets.publishing.service.gov.uk/government/uploads/system/uploads/attachment_data/file/812539/Schools_Pupils_and_their_Characteristics_2019_Main_Text.pdf.

Dix, Paul (2017). *When the Adults Change, Everything Changes: Seismic Shifts in School Behaviour* (Carmarthen: Independent Thinking Press).

Edelman, Marian Wright (2015). It's Hard to Be What You Can't See, *Children's Defense Fund* [blog] (21 August). Available at: https://www.childrensdefense.org/child-watch-columns/health/2015/its-hard-to-be-what-you-cant-see/.

Edge Foundation, The (2019). Localism Key to Addressing Skill Shortage Crisis, Says Edge Foundation (12 November). Available at: https://www.edge.co.uk/news/edge-news/skills-shortages-bulletin-6.

Eurostat (2020). Cultural Statistics Report (May). Available at: https://ec.europa.eu/eurostat/statistics-explained/index.php/Culture_statistics_-_cultural_employment#Self-employment.

Flores Chandler, Stacey (2019). Did JFK Say It?: 'One Person Can Make A Difference and Everyone Should Try', *The JFK Library Archives* [blog] (28 October). Available at: https://jfk.blogs.archives.gov/2019/10/28/make-a-difference-quote/.

Future First (2019). *Young People, Their Futures and Access to Relatable Role Models* (September). Available at: https://futurefirst.org.uk/blog/young-people-their-futures-and-access-to-relatable-role-models/.

Gatsby Charitable Foundation (2014). *Good Career Guidance* (London: Gatsby Charitable Foundation). Available at: https://www.gatsby.org.uk/uploads/education/reports/pdf/gatsby-sir-john-holman-good-career-guidance-2014.pdf.

Greenhouse Sports (2019). Annual Review 2018–19. Available at: https://www.greenhousesports.org/wp-content/uploads/2019/12/Greenhouse-Sports-Annual-Review-2018-19-Final.pdf.

Griffiths, Sian (2019). Oxbridge 'Penalises' Private School Pupils, *The Times* (25 August). Available at: https://thetimes.co.uk/article/oxbridge-penalises-private-school-pupils-m89dpbmqp.

Hickman, Arvind (2019). W Launches Social Enterprise to Fundamentally Change Industry's Talent Pipeline, *PR Week* (24 October). Available at: https://www.prweek.com/article/1663527/w-launches-social-enterprise-fundamentally-change-industrys-talent-pipeline.

Hooley, Tristram (2019). Can HE Single-Handedly Solve Skills Shortages? *WonkHE* [blog] (9 September). Available at: https://wonkhe.com/blogs/can-higher-education-single-handedly-solve-skills-shortages/.

Huffington, Arianna (2014). *Thrive: The Third Metric to Redefining Success and Creating a Happier Life* (London: WH Allen).

Hull LEP (2018). The Humber's Blueprint for an Industrial Strategy. Available at: https://www.humberlep.org/wp-content/uploads/2018/06/The-Humbers-Blueprint.pdf.

Jin, Wenchao, Alastair Muriel and Luke Sibieta (2010). *Subject and Course Choices at Ages 14 and 16 Amongst Young People in England: Insights from Behavioural Economics*. Research Report DFE-RR160 (May). Available at: https://assets.publishing.service.gov.uk/government/uploads/system/uploads/attachment_data/file/182677/DFE-RR160.pdf.

Jobs, Steve (2005). Stanford University Commencement Speech, 12 June. Available at: https://news.stanford.edu/2005/06/14/jobs-061505/.

Kerr, James (2013). *Legacy: What the All Blacks Can Teach Us about the Business of Life* (London: Constable).

King Jr, Martin Luther (1963). *Strength to Love* (New York: Harper & Row).

Knight, Magda (2018). Are Apprenticeships Worth It? 6 Questions You're Secretly Asking (And Their Myth-Busting Answers), *Youth Employment UK* (6 March). Available at: https://www.youthemployment.org.uk/are-apprenticeships-worth-it-myths-facts/.

McFadden, Cynthia and Jake Whitman (2014). Sheryl Sandberg Launches 'Ban Bossy' Campaign to Empower Girls to Lead, *ABC News* (10 March). Available at: https://abcnews.go.com/US/sheryl-sandberg-launches-ban-bossy-campaign-empower-girls/story?id=22819181.

Mann, Anthony (2012). It's Who You Meet: Why Employer Contacts at School Make a Difference to the Employment Prospects of Young Adults. Education and Employers Taskforce. Available at: https://www.educationandemployers.org/wp-content/uploads/2014/06/its_who_you_meet_final_26_06_12.pdf.

Mann, Anthony, Elnaz T. Kashefpakdel, Jordan Rehill and Prue Huddleston (2017). *Contemporary Transitions: Young Britons Reflect on Life After Secondary School and College*, Education and Employers Occasional Research Paper 11 (September). Available at: https://www.educationandemployers.org/wp-content/uploads/2017/01/Contemporary-Transitions-30-01-2017.pdf.

May, Theresa (2016). 'The Great Meritocracy: Prime Minister's Speech', 9 September. Available at: https://www.gov.uk/government/speeches/britain-the-great-meritocracy-prime-ministers-speech.

Montacute, Rebecca (2018). Internships: Unpaid, Unadvertised, Unfair. Sutton Trust research brief, edition 20 (January). Available at: https://www.suttontrust.com/research-paper/internships-unpaid-unadvertised-unfair/.

Nagdee, Ilyas (2019). 'Half-Truth Histories: How Erasing Empire Maintains the Status Quo'. In Nikesh Shukla and Sammy Jones (eds), *RIFE: Twenty-One Stories from Britain's Youth* (London: Unbound), pp. 193–209.

National Careers Week (2019). NCW Highlight Report. Available at: https://nationalcareersweek.com/download/16707/.

NHS Digital (2018). Measures from the Adult Social Care Outcomes Framework, England 2017–18 (23 October). Available at: https://digital.nhs.uk/data-and-information/publications/statistical/adult-social-care-outcomes-framework-ascof/current.

Office for National Statistics (2019). Disability and Employment, UK: 2019 [statistical release] (2 December). Available at: https://www.ons.gov.uk/peoplepopulationandcommunity/healthandsocialcare/disability/bulletins/disabilityandemploymentuk/2019#main-points.

Office for National Statistics (2020). Young People Not in Education, Employment or Training [statistical bulletin] (27 February). Available at: https://www.ons.gov.uk/employmentandlabourmarket/peoplenotinwork/unemployment/bulletins/youngpeoplenotineducationemploymentortrainingneet/february2020.

Ofsted (2016). *Getting Ready for Work*. Ref: 160056 (November). Available at: https://assets.publishing.service.gov.uk/government/uploads/system/uploads/attachment_data/file/577236/Getting_ready_for_work.pdf.

Ofsted (2020). *The Annual Report of Her Majesty's Chief Inspector of Education, Children's Services and Skills 2018/19*. Ref: HC 28 2018-19. Available at: https://assets.publishing.service.gov.uk/government/uploads/system/uploads/attachment_data/file/859422/Annual_Report_of_Her_Majesty_s_Chief_Inspector_of_Education__Children_s_Services_and_Skills_201819.pdf.

Owen, Jonathan (2018). Winners of the TES FE Awards 2018 Announced, *TES* (24 February). Available at: https://www.tes.com/news/winners-tes-fe-awards-2018-announced.

Percy, Christian, Jordan Rehill, Elnaz Kashefpakdel, Nick Chambers, Ashley Hodges and Max Haskins (2019). *Insight and Inspiration: Evaluating the Impact on Guest Speakers in Schools* (London: Education and Employers and Speakers4Schools). Available at: https://www.educationandemployers.org/wp-content/uploads/2019/10/Insights-and-Inspiration-Exploring-the-impact-of-guest-speakers-in-schools-1.pdf.

Perraudin, Frances (2019). GCSE Results Day 2019: Increase in Top Grades – Live, *The Guardian* (22 August). Available at: https://www.theguardian.com/education/live/2019/aug/22/gcse-results-day-2019-live-news.

Phillips, Jess (2017). *Everywoman: One Woman's Truth about Speaking the Truth* (London: Hutchinson).

Pinkett, Matt and Mark Roberts (2019). *Boys Don't Try? Rethinking Masculinity in Schools* (Abingdon and New York: Routledge).

Rayner, Angela (2016). We Must Be Serious About Vocational Education, *New Statesman – Spotlight, Skills: Training for the New Economy* (11 November). Available at: https://www.newstatesman.com/sites/default/files/skills_supplement_11th_nov_2016_0.pdf.

Royal Academy of Engineering (2019). *Engineering Skills for the Future: The 2013 Perkins Review Revisited*. Available at: www.raeng.org.uk/perkins2019.

Royal Society (2019). Royal Society Calls for Independent Review of Post-16 Education (12 February). Available at: https://royalsociety.org/news/2019/02/call-for-independent-review-of-post-16-education/.

Runswick-Cole, Katherine (2018). Education is not a Chocolate Biscuit. In Emma McGarry and Adam J. B. Walker (eds), *Special Rights* (London: Serpentine Galleries), pp. 13–15. Available at: https://www.serpentinegalleries.org/files/downloads/181114_special-rights-wholebook.pdf.

Sandberg, Sheryl (2013). *Lean In: Women, Work and the Will to Lead* (London: WH Allen).

Saunders, Frances (2013). *Closing Doors: Exploring Gender and Subject Choice in Schools*, An Institute of Physics report (December). Available at: http://www.iop.org/education/teacher/support/girls_physics/closing-doors/page_62076.html.

Sutton Trust and the Department for Business, Innovation and Skills (2009). *Applications, Offers and Admissions to Research-Led Universities,* BIS Research Paper No. 5 (August). Available at: https://www.suttontrust.com/wp-content/uploads/2019/12/BIS_ST_report-1.pdf.

Swindoll, Charles R. (1982). *Strengthening Your Grip* (London: Hodder and Stoughton).

Townsend, Chris (2019). Do You Mind the Gap? *This Week in FM* (5 March). Available at: https://www.twinfm.com/article/do-you-mind-the-gap.

UK Hospitality (2018). *UK Hospitality Workforce Commission 2030 Report: The Changing Face of Hospitality* (September). Available at: https://www.youthemployment.org.uk/dev/wp-content/uploads/2018/09/UK-Hospitality-Workforce-Commission-2030.pdf.

Unison (2016). NHS Exploiting Apprentices through Low Pay, Warns UNISON [press release] (24 April). Available at: https://www.unison.org.uk/news/press-release/2016/04/nhs-exploiting-apprentices-through-low-pay-warns-unison/.

Wagner, Tony (2008). *The Global Achievement Gap: Why Even Our Best Schools Don't Teach the New Survival Skills Our Children Need – and What We Can Do About It* (New York: Basic Books).

Washington, Booker T. (2015 [1901]). *Up from Slavery: An Autobiography* [Kindle edn].

Weale, Sally (2019). Poorer Pupils Twice as Likely to Fail Key GCSEs, *The Guardian* (21 August). Available at: https://www.theguardian.com/education/2019/aug/21/poorer-pupils-twice-as-likely-to-fail-key-gcses.

Whitmore, John (1992). *Coaching for Performance: A Practical Guide to Growing Your Own Skills* (London: Nicholas Brealey Publishing).

Young, Lord (2014). *Enterprise for All: The Relevance of Enterprise in Education* (June). Available at: https://assets.publishing.service.gov.uk/government/uploads/system/uploads/attachment_data/file/338749/EnterpriseforAll-lowres-200614.pdf.

Zecharia, Anna, Ellie Cosgrave, Liz Thomas and Rob Jones (2014). *Through Both Eyes: The Case for a Gender Lens in STEM*. Available at: https://sciencegrrl.co.uk/assets/SCIENCE-GRRL-Stem-Report_FINAL_WEBLINKS-1.pdf.

ABOUT THE AUTHOR

Andrew Bernard, or 'Bernie' to everyone who knows him, was a confirmed underachiever at school, preferring to be at the back of the class instead of engaging his brain. He left grammar school with an E and a U at A level, which you could say was a wake-up call. Luckily, UCAS clearing and his mum were on hand to help and he decided he needed to leave his hometown and went away to college in north Wales – one of only two options on offer.

After three successful years and a distinction in a business and finance HND, one of his testicles tried to kill him. Following a delicate operation and a course of chemotherapy he went on to work at Unilever and at management levels in a construction firm, the University of Salford (including lecturing part-time for the management school) and Lancaster University, taking a degree, postgrad certificate and teaching qualification part-time. Still feeling he was missing something and suffering from stress at work, he did a fire walk at 38 years old and decided he wanted to work with young people.

He started Innovative Enterprise in 2006, and so far Bernie and the company have delivered more than 1,800 workshops and talks internationally, working with over 150,000 people. Bernie is a director of National Careers Week, a Fellow of the Professional Speaking Association, a TEDx speaker and an entrepreneur. He has spoken internationally in the UK, Europe and the UAE, designed educational and corporate social responsibility challenges for FTSE 100 companies and global businesses, and he brings passion and enthusiasm to events as a speaker, MC or facilitator.

Bernie lives with his wife Val in rural north Lancashire and they have two adult daughters, Millie and Ruby. In his spare time Bernie enjoys cycling, reading, watching films and campervanning in Scotland and France.

@EnterpriseSBox

innovative enterprise

Bernie started Innovative Enterprise in 2006 after realising that a 'proper job' was neither conducive to his mental well-being nor something he particularly cared about. After much reflection, and with his wife's help, he decided he needed to be the person he himself had needed when he was younger: someone to motivate, inspire and enthuse young people into believing the future is full of excitement and possibility rather than a place where your dreams are often crushed by the mundanity of working in jobs you don't care about.

Innovative Enterprise's strapline is 'Bringing the future to life', and this is the one thread that weaves the workshops, talks and resources (and now this book) together under the Innovative Enterprise banner. The company delivers a variety of workshops – covering creativity, leadership, enterprise, risk, teamwork and motivation – for hundreds of people at a time in schools, colleges and universities, with a professional peripatetic team of facilitators.

Designing challenges for clients in education, FTSE 100 companies, global manufacturers and for National Careers Week is something that Bernie has always done under the Innovative Enterprise banner. He also delivers keynotes in person and virtually, which turn his and his family's experiences into powerful learning experiences for others.

More information and contact details can be found at www.innovativeenterprise.co.uk